D1557249

Gia!
May God bless you
to become a reconciler!

Brett Fuller (signature)

Dreaming IN
Black AND White

BRETT FULLER

ISBN (Print): 978-1-09838-741-9
ISBN (eBook): 978-1-09838-742-6

CONTENTS

I dedicate this book to:
My grandparents and parents who lived exemplary lives of conciliation.
My bride Cynthia who has sacrificed much to allow me to do much.
My children (Joseph, Brian, Garrison, Meredith, Telos, Brook and Grant)
who have lived their lives in a ministry fishbowl so dad could fulfill
his calling. Thank you all for being who you are and for doing
what you have done. Your accommodation fuels my life.

By Sinbad

I have had the pleasure of knowing Brett Fuller since he was a young man. My wife is one of three children, of which he is the eldest. When I first met Brett, it was very early in his ministerial career. He held services out of a brownstone on C Street in Washington, DC. Brett struck me as a proud black man, kind to his core yet very aware of the racial challenges that exist within the world and in his own personal experience as both a black man and a man of faith. At a time when we are grappling with the universal outrage and outcry over racial and social injustices existing in America, this book is much needed and right on time.

Although we share similar views about the racial inequities and injustices which have divided this country in recent years and rocked it to its core, the manner in which Brett and I choose to express our grievances couldn't be further apart. Until recently, I was always a knee jerk reaction type of guy who fired off in anger when it came to issues of racism. I spoke from a place of pain—a characteristic I know many of you can relate to after witnessing the countless, senseless murders of innocent black men and women of late. Some of these happened right before our eyes. Most were without a shred of remorse or accountability.

Yet what I admire about Brett is his unique ability to consider and characterize an issue prior to returning a well thought out response drawn from the wisdom he receives from God that promotes education, healing and restoration. When he speaks, peace fills your spirit. That's why *Dreaming in Black and White* is an important and necessary read. I dare to imagine a world beyond its pages.

There is power in our stories. It is in sharing the tales of our ancestors, our beloved ones who have come and gone, that we unlock the beauty of God's lens and intention for His people, divinely and purposefully created in our unique skin. Our stories outline the glory of legacy, as well as the fight which has allowed us to arrive at this current moment. These stories tell us where we have come from and provide a pathway for us to pick up the mantle and continue to march forward. *Dreaming in Black and White* is a model for what it looks like to share our stories, bravely and proudly. For it is in our collective storytelling that we can begin to step into understanding, into acceptance, into love. And, once there is love, there is no fight we cannot brave together.

Brett delves into the issues of racial inequality from a deeply personal perspective while also taking us through the generational pain of a past that doesn't look so different from present days. The way he acquaints us with the effects and perils of racist mindsets and behaviors, be it intentional or not, by both reflectively sharing events from his personal life and historical veracity, allows for us, as the readers, to come into a space that is both enlightening and sacred. There is beauty in the way he communicates the harsh and ugly truths of what has kept us apart and divided us in this country, kept us from embodying "on earth as it is in heaven," with bold transparency and daring vulnerability.

Most poignantly, behind every declarative truth of our past and present, is his ability to courageously and boldly hope for a better tomorrow—a tomorrow that is guided and marked by the heart of Jesus. He proposes a solution centered in Jesus Christ that exposes the idea that to God, there is nothing new under the sun. His proposal of racial reconciliation as not solely an end result but the means by which we achieve true brotherly and sisterly love in Christ is both radically thought-provoking and inspiring.

America and its inhabitants have existed far too long on different pages when it comes to detailing the characteristics that make this country great. When we speak about racial reconciliation, there is often an aversion to sitting in the discomfort of revealing and acknowledging what, for blacks and other BIPOC people in America, have experienced as a fragmented and complicated American experience. There are many who would much rather leave the past in the past.

Brett impels us to recognize that we cannot remove the chains of our past until we are willing to take ownership of the ugly, harmful pieces of the American story. He challenges us to consider the fact that we can only begin to reconstruct that which we acknowledge is broken. Only then can we blaze a path anew. Through his illustrative words, Brett appeals to our greater call as a humanity. He calls us to not simply co-exist, but rather invite one another into kinship, echoing the call of leaders before him such as Martin Luther King Jr. who has said, "We must learn to live together as brothers or perish together as fools."

Every page takes you on a compelling journey of identity, historical mapping, and Biblical discernment. Each word holds more than just an education. It holds an awakening—an awakening of thought, of emotions, of a personal and spiritual responsibility to act. Brett ends with an encouraging word to the generations who walk behind us—who have watched their leaders sworn to protect instead incite racism and vilify the innocent in real time—to not lose heart. He calls them to continue to fight the good fight, to utilize their youth, creativity, and resources to make their voices heard, to believe they, indeed, are the chosen ones.

If you want to understand the anger of black people or why we shout "Black Lives Matter," this book is a must read. If you want to learn how to best walk out God's heart for injustice, for the oppressed, this book is a must read. I don't believe a single one of us, after reading this book, will be able to ignore the conviction that lies in the depth of its pages. I am grateful a book like this exists. It models the art of bold truth-telling and captures the heart and vision of God for His Church, for His people. Thank you, brother Brett, for your words, for your wisdom, and for your action in a time such as this.

PROLOGUE

From the time when men called caves their homes, images sketched on walls told stories, tales that ranged from hunting conquests to everyday life. Most of these drawings were done with pigments extracted from earthy minerals such as iron oxide and coal, thus the oft seen colors of red and black inside caves.

As time marched on, talented people with an exceptional eye for beauty brought life to canvas in every color imaginable. In vivid detail, Rembrandt, Leonardo da Vinci, and Michelangelo portrayed the world through the artistry of their brush.

These masters and their masterpieces achieved world-wide fame, yet their depictions of reality took weeks to create, if not years. Men began to question: How do we create a way to capture life's moments more quickly? Finally, a breakthrough came in the 1800's when inventors and scientists created the first process that could record the detail of life's moments in minutes.

In 1820, French inventor Nicephore Niépce became the first man to capture a fixed image with a camera. The developing process required up to eight hours, and the resulting image was a crude black and white photo, yet Niépce had broken through. In 1839, Niépce's associate, artist Louis Daguerre, furthered Niépce's work by creating the daguerreotype process, the first commercially viable photographic process. For the first time, humanity was able to catch visual life quickly, accurately, and repeatedly.

Forty years later, on June 19th, 1878, Eadweard Muybridge, having been contracted by Leland Stanford (the founder of Stanford University), used twelve separate cameras to film a man riding a horse on the Palo Alto Stock Farm (the eventual site of Stanford University). Only eleven shots from those twelve cameras were spliced together to produce the first motion picture (book cover). This moving image proved, among other things, that a horse running in full stride briefly has all four legs off the ground. The film was shot in black-and-white and was the beginning of all that is cinema today.

Hold this truth in your mind: it took both black and white in concert to capture the truth—of a horse running, of daily life, of all that we now see on the many screens of our lives. At first, though, it took both black and white.

In August of 1963, Dr. Martin Luther King Jr. trumpeted his famous "I Have A Dream Speech" from the steps of the Lincoln Memorial. Those who misunderstood Dr. King thought he was only claiming civil rights for the black man. No doubt he was, but he was also attempting to apprehend more. He was calling all Americans to a higher bar of liberty and justice.

Regarding his desire for black and white people to dwell together in harmony, he said,

"I have a dream… one day right there in Alabama, little black boys and black girls will be able to join hands with little white boys and white girls as sisters and brothers.

He also advocated for America to live up to the words penned by her founding fathers. In the same speech he said,

"I have a dream that one day this nation will rise up and live out the true meaning of its creed, "We hold these truths to be self-evident, that all men are created equal."

Dr. King was dreaming, but not just in one color. He was dreaming in black and white. He wanted the greatest relational/ethnic rift in our nation's history to be healed. Although he would rejoice for every Kodak moment that evidenced progress—a Jim Crow "whites only" sign being pulled down by a white man, a black child breaking the color barrier by transferring to a white school—he would not be satisfied with a singular incident. He wanted to facilitate the creation of a unending film depicting ethnic unity and harmony. It would be a masterpiece made in the boroughs of New York City and stretching to beaches of San Diego. Indeed, from Portland, Oregon, to Atlanta, Georgia, he wanted America to be a big-screen cinematic production that could show how humanity was intended to work best. If he was able to help repair the issues between the black and white people of America, similar issues embedded in other international ethnic struggles could be addressed with corresponding results.

This book, *Dreaming in Black and White,* is all about believing for, creating, and capturing iconic moments of resolve and healing. It is about leveraging and connecting those moments in a frame-by-frame continuum so that the beautiful revelation of ongoing unity and sociological health become undeniable results of the sacrifice made to produce them. It is about understanding the fears, confusion, and concerns of the white population, while rightly processing the deep pain of the black. It will present a way to inform the ignorant without being offended by their ignorance, how to lead with mercy in a way that never bypasses truth and justice. How to listen. How to give people a piece of your heart, when you desperately want to give them a piece of your mind. How to grow from being just a point-maker to a peace-maker.

Dreaming in Black and White will make the reader hunger to develop the conciliatory skills that resist the mistrust and bitterness that abide in the soul of the offended. It will also instill the necessary steadfastness to be doggedly mission-focused until the pricking of our national conscience produces a multiethnic people who are happily and equally joined together Americans.

Every day of my American life I dream in black and white. Everyday of my church life I dream in color, but this book is largely written to help the black reader build a bridge to the white, and visa versa. The forces against this dream are many. Still, I strain forward against the headwinds that would keep both people groups—black and white—from becoming whole, healed, and unified. I would like to arrive one day at the place where I could dream only in color—a dream that focuses on every nation, tongue and tribe gathering in unity to fulfill God's hope for humanity in the world; but I am just one man, with one life, and with one mission from God: help heal my nation. Thus, until there is no longer the need to carry the unfulfilled hopes, pain, and confusion of black and white folks, I will pray, sacrifice, speak, write, weep, and intercede for America.

As you journey with me through my story, and America's story, I pray that you will have at least one photographic moment that, when attached to mine, can help produce a cinematic masterpiece.

THE MEANING OF
THIS MOMENT

—————————————————

I write these words in the year 2020. If this book is still being read in a hundred years, I want my future readers to know that I wrote in the midst of this terrible, transitional year. Not all authors have felt this way. Charles Dickens likely did not care that *A Christmas Carol* was written in 1843 as opposed to any other year, and Maya Angelou probably felt the same about releasing *I Know Why the Caged Bird Sings* in 1969. Yet everything I have to say in the pages that follow springs from the great urgencies of 2020.

It is a year of global pandemic and economic upheaval. It is a season of perhaps the dirtiest political warfare the United States has ever known. It is a time of fear and uncertainty, of destruction and loss. I write now, though, because of another facet of this fateful year. I write because it was in this year that the cup of unrighteously shed black blood overflowed—and much of the world took notice and said, "No more!"

This came in the wake of a long series of black deaths at the hands of police. In these, most of the victims were unarmed. Most were already in police custody. Most proved later to be innocent of the deeds that brought them under suspicion. Each of these incidents fell like hammer blows upon the national consciousness. They are troubling to even think about. Still, if we hope to courageously heal, we must first courageously face the disease that makes the healing necessary.

In 2014, Eric Garner died after being wrestled to the ground by New York police officers. Garner was suspected of illegally selling cigarettes on the street. While gripped in a policeman's choke hold, Garner uttered the words "I can't breathe" eleven times. Then, he breathed no more.

In that same year, Michael Brown, aged eighteen, was killed by Ferguson, Missouri, police after he was suspected of stealing a box of cigars. Though unarmed, he was shot six times.

Also in 2014, Tamir Rice, twelve years old, was killed by Cleveland, Ohio, police after the boy pointed a toy gun at an officer.

In 2015, Walter Scott of Charleston, South Carolina, was pulled over by police for a broken taillight. There was a scuffle and Walter reportedly tried to run. He was shot in the back five times before he died.

In 2016, Philando Castile was driving with his girlfriend in St. Paul, Minnesota, when police pulled the couple's car over in a routine traffic stop. Philando informed officers he had a weapon and possessed a license to do so. It didn't matter. When he reached for his driver's license as officers had asked him to do, he was shot to death.

In 2018, Stephon Clark was shot seven times in Sacramento, California, because police who were investigating an armed robbery said they feared for their lives. Stephon was standing in his grand-mother's backyard at the time, talking on a cell phone. Though he was unarmed, the police fired at him more than twenty times.

In 2019, Atatiana Jefferson, twenty-eight, was shot and killed by Fort Worth, Texas, police while she sat in her living room with her eight-year-old nephew. The shots were fired through the window of her home. Police were responding to a call from a neighbor that Atatiana's door had been left open.

Also in 2019, Elijah McClain, twenty-three, died in police cus-tody in Aurora, Colorado, after he was reported for wearing a ski mask and looking "sketchy." Police pinned Elijah to the ground, put him in a choke hold, and then involved paramedics who injected enough ket-amine into McClain for a man twice his size. Among Elijah's last words in this world were those telling the police that he loved them.

In 2020, Breonna Taylor, a twenty-six-year-old emergency med-ical technician, was shot eight times when Louisville, Kentucky, police raided her apartment while executing a search warrant. None of the suspected drugs were found.

Also in 2020, Minneapolis police arrested George Floyd on suspi-cion of passing counterfeit currency. During the arrest, an officer held Floyd to the ground by putting a knee on his neck for approximately nine minutes. Floyd complained that he was claustrophobic and that he couldn't breathe. He suffocated to death.

That same year, Jacob Blake was shot seven times in the back by Kenosha, Wisconsin, police. Blake's girlfriend—the mother of his chil-dren—had called the police because she and Blake presumably were having an intense disagreement. He was shot while trying to enter a car where his children were sitting.

Then there was Ahmaud Arbery. He was jogging in a Brunswick, Georgia, neighborhood when an ex-policeman and his son decided that Ahmaud was guilty of a string of recent neighborhood break-ins. The two tracked down the twenty-six-year-old and shot him to death. Investigators later confirmed that Ahmaud had nothing to do with the break-ins.

There were more. There will be more. Botham Jean was eating ice cream in his Dallas living room. Eric Reason was arriving at a chicken and fish shop. Dominique Clayton was sleeping in her bed. Ezell Ford was walking in his neighborhood. All were shot and killed by police. All were black.

Commissions sat. Investigations were authorized. Suspensions and firings were announced and charges were brought. Protests swirled and cities burned.

Yet something more was happening. Beyond the headlines, beyond the agony of each individual incident, there was a broader sense descending upon the nation. It was a sense of reckoning. It was as though the record of the nation's ills, a long legacy of racism, and the exhausting, painful journey of black America all converged in this destined year. Somehow a resolve arose, a determination—born of righteous indignation and more than a little weariness—that it all had to change. That the bloodshed and the bitterness could not again be passed along to the next generation.

It was not just black America that felt this moment come upon them. It seemed to be all willing and righteous souls. White grand-mothers joined arms with black teenagers. Peaceful protestors were often more white or Asian or Hispanic than black. Kurds from half a world away tweeted their support and completely white professional hockey teams refused to play in order to support mostly black pro basketball teams. Something was happening. Something was felt. And not by blacks alone.

So, a bit of hope—faint and unsteady—began to emerge from this tragic year.

I came to this moment in time as a Christian leader—the pastor of a larger than small church near Washington, DC, the chaplain of the NFL's Washington Football Team, and a leader in an international network of churches. As important, I also came as a black man, one who has suffered his own indignities and who felt the racial horrors of 2020 keenly.

I admit I had a different perspective than most. My life had long been defined by three truths that set me apart and allowed me to work for healing as the troubles of 2020 arose. First, I had been transformed by the truth that there is a God and that he is a God of love who is reaching to each of us and to all our institutions in order to heal and restore. Second, I had been healed and set on fire by the realization that this same God made me a black man for his purposes, just as surely as he has made people of all ethnicities, skin colors, and nationalities to serve his purposes on earth. And, finally, I had been transfixed by the understanding that this God enthrones himself in heaven among all the earthly nations, tribes, people groups, and languages he has made. He loves them. He enjoys them. He revels in their splendor and their praise. He is calling them to himself.

So the lens through which I have perceived this troubling year and, in fact, the basis of my whole life's work, has been defined by the prayer of Jesus in what we have come to call The Lord's Prayer: "Your will be done on earth as it is in heaven." This, I know, is the answer for our time. It is the healing balm for the racial wounds and injustices that sever us. It is the purpose for which we are created and it leads to the grace that will allow us to be the unified people we are made to be.

As confidently as I say this, I know also that religion has often been more a problem than the solution in the matter of racial justice. Many churches have slept through social crises. Worse, historically they have allowed organizations like the Ku Klux Klan to hide behind them. Churchmen have distorted the scriptures and their own souls to justify sinful paths. I know this and oppose such wrongs wherever I can.

I also know that the attempt to counterfeit a truth does not deny that truth. I still believe, then—in God, in what he has said, in what he can do, and in his loving purposes that can set us right again.

This brings us to these pages. Here, I plan to speak plainly in the confidence that the truth sets us free. I will tell my own story, tell a bit of the story of black America, and then offer the wisdom I've acquired by grace and experience to help us begin to end the evil and build a society of racial justice and peace. Always my prayer and my purpose is, "Oh God, may your will be done on earth as it is being done in heaven."

Come with me, then. Defy the fear. Repent of the hate. Aggressively love. Lead with mercy. Realize the meaning of our times. And let us together seek to fulfill the hopes that the crises of 2020 cry out for.

CHAPTER 1

AMONG BUT
SELDOM A PART

have spent much of my life pressed between two worlds. I am a black man, one who has not only lived mostly in white society but who has also been called upon my whole life to explain the black world to the white, the white world to the black. It has not been easy. I long ago accepted this as the calling of God for my life, and I am grateful. But there has been a price. I want you to know this price, and so I want to take you with me on some of the journey I have known. Perhaps this will bring understanding. Perhaps it will lead to healing. My greatest hope is that it will help to both explain and to calm the desperate ethnic storms of our generation.

I must say at the start that my experience has not been on the most jagged edge of the black experience in America. My house has never been burned. No family member has ever been lynched. No man has been shot, no woman raped, no child kidnapped or maimed among my immediate relations. I have never been pummeled by police or dragged down a gravel road by men in white sheets or taunted by an angry racist crowd. Many who look like me have known such horrors.

No, my experience in America is far more normal. Perhaps that is the tragedy.

I was fortunate to be born to two proud African American parents. They both understood and reveled in the glory of being black. They both chose to attend Historically Black Colleges and Universities (HBCUs), but their choice was systemically corralled because they did not ethnically qualify to attend their major State universities. Still, the education they enjoyed was in no way less-than.

They both were skilled professionals. They both had a profound understanding of justice and truth. They both also knew the story of their people and the power that black heritage meant for their time. I was the beneficiary of all of this. How very grateful I am.

My mother, Violaruth Joyce Johnson, was an amazing woman. She was born in St. Louis, Missouri, in 1937, to a father who worked food service on the railroad and a mother who was a nurse. She thrived in the public schools of her city and then attended and graduated from Lincoln University in Jefferson City, Missouri in the Spring of 1958 and earned her Masters in Education from Tuskegee Institute in 1971.

In 1958, she took a job in the Kansas City school system. It was a difficult job at a difficult time in our nation's history and it was all the more so for a black woman. My mother did it and did it well. What a legacy she left me. I don't mind telling you that my mother was beautiful. That's not just a proud son talking. You can see for yourself.

Violaruth Joyce Johnson

With another student she appeared on the cover of the March issue of *Ebony* magazine in 1958.

If I am accused of bragging, guilty as charged. I am unapologetically proud of my heritage!

My father, Joseph Everett Fuller Jr. sprang from far different soil. He was born in 1930 in Tuskegee, Alabama.

Dr. Joseph Everett Fuller Jr.

His father, my grandfather, was the head of the math department at the famed Tuskegee Institute, now Tuskegee University, the groundbreaking school founded by Booker T. Washington. As if that wasn't accomplishment enough, my grandfather was also the president of the Tuskegee Savings and Loan. My grandmother Ruby died of breast cancer in 1955, so in 1960 my grandfather married Rosa Arrington, a regal woman who was a professor in the English department at Tuskegee.

It was easy to write the words you see in this previous paragraph. It was much harder to live those words. Imagine what it was like for my grandfather to achieve what he did. He graduated from what is now

Bradley University in 1929 and went on to earn his Master of Arts in Mathematics from the University of Michigan in 1929 and his PhD from the University of Pennsylvania in 1945.

Of course, 1929, the year Joseph Fuller Sr. graduated from college, was the year during which the Great Depression began. It was also during the Jim Crow era. "Separate but equal" was the law of the land. It was a cruel joke. Blacks were still being lynched. Racism ruled. That blacks would ride in the back of the train or the bus and step off the sidewalk when a white person approached was still expected in much of the country. Despite it all, my grandfather had earned his MA and PhD at two prominent universities in the North and had then chosen to serve his people at a school in the deep South. What a man he was. What a hero he has always been to me.

His experience left scars. We can only imagine together how many times he was called "n----r" or "boy"—despite the fact he was an accomplished man, certainly far better educated than those who abused him. We can try to envision the moments he was threatened or refused service or perhaps humiliated in front of the woman he loved. We cannot know exactly how this felt to him.

I do know some of the impact of these injustices upon him because I remember from my earliest days hearing him say that he would never go to the white part of Tuskegee. He said he had no intention of giving his money to white people. He would keep his business in the black community. Even when segregation ended, Grandpa never went to the white side of town, so torturous was the treatment he had endured, so deeply wounding were the injustices.

My grandfather had his disappointments but also his inspirations. He believed deeply in his students and in what they promised for the future. There he was just two generations from slavery, training gifted young black students to go out and change the world. I've always imagined they inspired him and that this was a hedge against the pain and the mistreatment. He also knew the eccentric inventor George Washington Carver, whom he admired. Still, seeing such black geniuses serving humanity by way of serving God surely changed him. He became, in time, a man of deep faith and I am grateful for that legacy in my family.

My father grew up in Tuskegee, then, and he, too, became an accomplished man. His was a far more exotic story than his own father's, though. Dad attended Tuskegee High School and was a gifted student and athlete. Again, I may be bragging, but I have good reason. In 1947, just as Jackie Robinson was breaking the color barrier in professional baseball, the Philadelphia Phillies were looking at my father as a possible part of their team.

Unfortunately, it was just as athletic opportunities loomed to join a Major League squad, that my father received a draft notice from the Air Force. He decided to defer his enlistment and go to college. He enrolled at Lincoln University in Philadelphia. There, he studied. He played baseball. He drank deeply from the noble black culture at that stellar HBCU. One of the treasures from Dad's life that we still hold dear in my family is his yearbook from Lincoln University. In it, his coach wrote, "I have never seen a better baseball player in my life." The words mean a great deal to us even now and still speak of the possibilities that went unfulfilled in my father's life.

As he graduated from Lincoln, the Korean War was just beginning. Dad wanted to serve but he yearned to make a contribution, like his father, as a professional, at a more specialized level than as a common soldier or airman. He decided to train as a dentist and enrolled at the famed Meharry Medical School in Nashville, Tennessee, one of the most esteemed black medical schools in the country. He graduated in 1954 with his dentistry degree and then enlisted in the Air Force in 1954-55. He would serve as a military dentist for two years. It was during this time that Dad's story, well, just takes an odd turn.

It seems that during Dad's military years, he returned while on leave to Tuskegee to spend time with his best friends from high school. They went to a night club that hosted live musical artists. In the way of often-told family stories, the details always survive. That the beer that night was two dollars a pitcher is something I know because this detail was repeated time and again throughout my life. While the guys were celebrating and horsing around, one of the buddies suddenly turned to my dad and said, "I dare you to get up on that stage and sing a song." Well, there weren't many challenges my Joe Fuller did not accept. Dad got up, sang beautifully, and sat down.

That would have been the end of the story except that there was a talent agent in the bar that night. He approached Dad and told him he was great and that fame as a singer was possible. He also asked if Dad would go to Memphis and record a demo. Dad agreed. Two weeks later, on the strength of that demo, Dad got a recording contract with Hi Records, a soul music and rockabilly label there in Memphis. Hi Records was the same label that signed the great Al Green years later, and released many of his hits, including *Let's Stay Together* and *Tired of Being Alone.*

My dad's season of fame began right then. I still have the vinyl 45 singles. They are invaluable mementos! He was on the road for a year and a half during 1958 and 1959, performing his singles like *You Made a Hit* and *Nothing But You.* He was such an impressive singer that his name—Joe Fuller—became well known. He even appeared on the *Tonight Show* with Jack Paar. That was real fame in those days! He also did concerts and was the warmup act for a number of well-known artists.

Finally, it all wound down, and Dad found himself in Kansas City pondering his future. It was then that he connected with an older dentist who was part of a previous generation of Meharry graduates. The man wanted to retire and offered Dad a chance to buy his practice. This was quite an opportunity. The man had a successful, ready-made practice that Dad could easily step into and take to new heights. The two made a deal and it proved to be a perfect move for both of them.

Dad brought new energy to the dental practice and began marketing in unique ways. He developed the then novel practice, for example, of going to the area elementary and high schools and conducting dental hygiene classes. He knew this would mean more clients over time. This is significant in my life because it was while Dad was doing a class at a school in Kansas City that he met Mom.

Now Mom and Dad may have been happy about their first meetings, but Grandma Johnson was not. She didn't like this young man who was interested in her daughter and she would slam the door every time he came around the house. I can imagine why this was true. First, Dad was too slick, handsome, and famous—quite the ladies' man. I imagine this might have scared any deeply Christian parents who saw him coming for their daughter. In addition, Dad had been married before. In fact, he had a son, my half-brother. So Grandma resisted all she could.

Still, Dad was a charmer. He showed up each week with roses and even made appearances at Mom's school. I imagine the neighbors weighed in on Dad's behalf because he was famous in the black community. Whatever Grandma's hesitations, they obviously dissolved over time. Mom and Dad were married six months after meeting, in June of 1959, and I was born eighteen months later in December of 1960.

Now, I have told you all this detail about my parents lives before I was even born because I want you to understand who they were. I think you can see that they were the kind of people any nation should want. They were professionals in their fields, working in education and healthcare. They met needs in people's lives and made contributions to the arts. They were good. There were productive. They were citizens.

But they were black, and this more than any of their other wonderful traits determined how they were treated in the years I'm about to describe. If you are black, you can already guess what is coming. If you are white, you likely have no clue that there are millions of stories like mine—and far worse. If you are Asian or Hispanic or Native American or some other ethnicity, you'll likely find an echo of your experience in the path my family and I have walked. It is time for our stories to be known and for them to help fashion a new day in this country and throughout the world.

I was born, then, when my parents were living in the 'hood of Kansas City. Growing up where I did and as I did all seemed quite normal to me. The people in my community were black. The people in my school were black. The people in my church were black. We stood together and looked with suspicion and not a little fear at the outer, white world. Still, as I say, it all seemed normal to me. I played with friends in the neighborhood. Their parents treated me like I was their own, just as my parents did their children. To say it in brief, I belonged. I was home.

Change came on the wings of two unpleasant events. The first occurred one day in 1964 when after I had finished playing a pickup game of baseball across the street, I turned and started to walk home. The owner of the home owned a massive Labrador Retriever. The dog noticed I was leaving the property, and for some reason decided to chase me. Realizing that my home was farther away than the time it took for the dog to catch me, I ran as fast as my four-year-old legs could carry me. I had that dog beat, too, all the way across the street, into my yard, and almost to the door of my house. I say almost, because it was in my yard that the dog caught up with me and bit me good. It wasn't just a nip, either. He tore open my jeans and drew blood. Ouch!

It's my father's reaction you have to keep your eye on. He was incensed! I remember he walked around the house demanding to know how this could happen when his son was playing just across the street in his own neighborhood. It upset him terribly and to my young mind the whole incident took on a larger meaning to my dad than it did to me.

Then an even worse thing happened. A policeman who lived in the neighborhood returned home one evening and absentmindedly left his loaded revolver on a table. The man had a little boy who was so young and inexperienced he did not even know what the revolver was. But with the curiosity of a child, the boy picked up the gun. Then he showed it to a five-year-old friend. The policeman's son ended up shooting his friend and killing him.

Now, the whole neighborhood was horrified and grief-stricken, but for my father that was the end. To him, our neighborhood had simply become too dangerous. The only way to secure his family's safety was to move. So, in the summer of 1966, my father relocated our family to the suburbs of Kansas City, Kansas, to a community called Leawood. I'm sure in my father's mind he was doing the right thing for his family. Leawood was upscale. It was prosperous. The schools were excellent. All was inviting and safe. I would soon start to wonder, though, if Dad had noticed that nearly everyone in Leawood was white. I had certainly noticed, and it was at this time, when I was just six, that I began to live between two worlds.

Dad bought a home for us. This should have been an easy thing for a prosperous dentist whose wife was an educator. It wasn't. No realtor would sell to a black man back then. No neighborhood like Leawood wanted a black family in their midst. I remember clearly that Dad had to buy our house directly from an owner and that he had to pay about 30 percent more for the privilege. Still, to my father's everlasting credit, he paid more because he wanted us to be safe.

Now, you might think that I'm about to tell you that we were shot at and our house was burned and there were riots in the streets because my black family took up residence in Leawood. Not so. The good citizens of Leawood were far too polite—publicly—to express themselves in such ways. Behind the scenes and under cover of darkness was another story.

You see, the 1960s were not a good time for black Americans. Neither, by the way, were the 1950s or the 1940s or the 1930s. White folks were afraid of the "dark." When the families in our neighborhoods turned on their televisions, what they saw were the riots. Black folks were up in arms. Inner cities were burning. Police were seen on the news beating blacks with nightsticks and shoving them handcuffed into paddy wagons or police vans. The overall message nice suburban white folks must have gotten at the time was this: blacks are bad. They are bent on destroying our society. They are outsiders come to do harm. Beware! These dark folks are dangerous.

We should remember that most Americans had no positive images of black Americans to look to in the early 1960s. Dr. Martin Luther King Jr. was well-known but he was highly controversial. America often saw him on the evening news coming or going from jail or leading some disturbing march. The television show *I Spy* was one of the first programs to feature a cool, capable, leading black figure, but it didn't start to air until 1965. I could go on. The point is that for most white Americans in the early 1960s, blacks were either poor, uneducated servants or dangerous radicals. Whatever they were, they should be treated with suspicion and opposed—particularly if they tried to live down the street from you.

I arrived for my first day of school in August of 1966. The other kids looked at me like I would mean the destruction not only of their school but of all that they loved. As a result, I had no friends that first year. In fact, had it not been for the graciousness of one dear woman, I would never even have entered anyone else's house that year. Her name was Mrs. Hague, my first grade teacher at Marsha Bagby Elementary School. Every single week, this stellar teacher—perhaps sensing my loneliness and seeing my family's isolation—came to my home to report to my mother about how I was doing in school. I remember thinking that this was simply what teachers did. I supposed my teachers would be giving my mother personal, weekly reports all my life. Of course, that was foolish, but it was a thought inspired by the kindness and care of Mrs. Hague, who made the first-grade experience of one lonely black kid a little less torturous.

There was another woman who made a difference in my life at the time and I have to pay her tribute. Her name was Mrs. Robinson. During my second grade year, she held a Bible study for kids my age after school each day and, fortunately, her son Tim broke through my isolation and invited me into the Robinson home. It was there that I first heard that my sins were an offense to God, that the blood of Jesus could cleanse that sin away, and that there was a thing called salvation for those who welcomed a man named Jesus into their lives, a man who had been brutalized on a cross long ago. I was captivated. I gave my life to Jesus and fully drank in all the truth my seven-year-old soul could absorb. Thankfully, Tim Robinson became my first friend.

Women like Mrs. Robinson and Mrs. Hague were harbors in the choppy seas of disdain that my family and I had to traverse. Though no one shouted at us or threatened us, the good citizens of Leawood made their rage at our color known in other ways. Our house was regularly egged. We woke up often to everything in our yard having been completely wrapped in toilet paper. It was a mess to clean up. I was also told that there was a cross burned in our neighborhood, though I never saw it. The message was clear. We could imagine the thinking of the perpetrators: "Let's show these uppity coloreds what we think of them. Let's drive them back across the tracks."

My mother once owned a 1964 Mustang. I'm telling you, it was gorgeous. It was cherry orange, had a stylish rag top, and sported the coolest hubcaps I'd ever seen. We woke up one morning to find it destroyed. The sides were bashed in. The ragtop was slashed, as were the tires. The seats were torn out and the windows were shattered. Someone had done a thorough job of demolishing that beautiful car.

I got in my share of fights at school. I lost most of them, but each of them was worth the scuffle. Many an afternoon I ran home in tears. "Why do we have to live here?" I would cry. "I don't like it here. Can we go back?" Of course, in my naivete and pain I didn't know how dangerous the inner city had become in those days. I just wanted to escape the agony of a black child in the white suburbs.

What tortured me most was why they hated me so much. I would lay in my bed and turn this over and over in my mind. Like most every black child in the world, I looked in the mirror and tried to figure out what they found so repulsive about me that they would treat me in such horrible ways. In his famous *Letter from Birmingham Jail*, Dr. King movingly described what forms in a child's "mental sky" when they are made to suffer bigotry and rejection merely for their color. Well, in those years, my mental sky was darkening. Clouds of bitterness and self-doubt were forming.

But why? Why should any child be made to cry themselves to sleep because they are so despised, and merely for the way God made them? There is only one answer and it is as simple as it is unjust. It was because we were black. It was because of the pigment of our skin, no matter our character or contributions to society. That was excuse enough to justify a deluge of evil visited upon us and all who looked like us.

I should tell you that during this time my parents were heroic. When I would run home crying from an insult or after another fight, not once did Mom and Dad encourage bitterness or speak ill of white people. They taught me to stay calm, to realize the good I was doing by being a standout student, a competitive athlete, and a willing friend. They also taught me, by their inspiring example, how to live courageously and how to be a "thriving-through-the-pain peacemaker."

There was an incident I recall in particular, one that must have been repeated millions of times around the United States. Our family wanted to enjoy the swimming pool at the Leawood Country Club. It was not too much to ask. Dad was more than willing to pay the fees necessary for his children to enjoy a summer dip. Still, we were refused. Dad appealed. We were refused again.

For most people that would have been the end of the story. Rejection would have won the day. Wounds would have deepened. Souls would have been tortured. And every hot day would have been another slap in the face with the renewed realization that people with black skin weren't allowed to share the cool waters with their neighbors.

It was at that moment that my father rose up and did something that has been an example of forward thinking and compassion for me ever since. He built a swimming pool in our backyard. Yes, he did! By God's grace, my parents had a bit of prosperity and they decided to use some of their wealth to show love to their kids and erect a barrier against the fiery darts of race hatred. That swimming pool was the first backyard pool in our neighborhood. Dad not only provided for us, but for all the white parents who couldn't afford the fee required for their kids to swim in Leawood Country Club's pool. In one magnificent deed my father reversed the situation, making his family no longer the hated exiles but the respected—or at least envied—owners of the only back-yard pool in the area. Such was the stuff of which my father was made.

My mother was heroic too and in a way that changed me forever. As a public school teacher herself, she knew what we weren't going to be learning about black history in school. To make up for that loss, she started turning our breakfast times before school into lessons about our black heritage. While we buttered our toast and chewed our eggs, she read Phillis Wheatley poems to us and taught us facts like that Wheatley was the first African American author of a book of poetry, a woman who wrote so beautifully that even George Washington praised her work. There were also lessons about Harriet Tubman, "the Black Moses," who rescued many slaves through the Underground Railroad.

I learned in my youth about people most Americans had never even heard of. There was Benjamin Banneker, self-taught mathematician and natural historian, who assisted in surveying the District of Columbia, wrote bestselling almanacs, and even corresponded with Thomas Jefferson, who was impressed with Banneker's encyclopedic knowledge. There was Crispus Attucks and George Washington Carver and Booker T. Washington and dozens of others who peopled my young imagination.

What was happening to me during these breakfast sessions was that I was being given a heritage. I was being shown who my people were and, therefore, who I was. I might have had to fight my way out of school, endure the isolation, and help my father clean up the yard after yet another act of vandalism, but all the while I was learning that I was descended from giants. My people were magnificent! What's more, their genius, their ingenuity, their raw courage and endurance lived in me. My mother built in me a fortress of understanding that allowed me to withstand all the slings and arrows of racial hatred, that allowed me to emerge inwardly unscathed from the forces that sought to tell me that I was not even human. Thank God for every poem I had to memorize, every paper I had to write, every breakfast lesson I sat through when barely awake.

While my parents taught me these lofty things, they also taught me the practical skills of being a black man in America. I knew that when I went into a department store I should keep my hands out of my pockets and speak to everyone with ultimate respect. I knew how to answer a policeman so he could see I meant no harm. My parents taught me how to be confident while carefully avoiding putting a white person on the defensive. These and a thousand other skills my parents burned into my young mind.

They wanted me to know the glory of being black while also knowing that the society in which we lived was not welcoming of who we were. We must know ourselves and protect ourselves. We must know our history but live among a people who were ignorant of that history. We must dwell among them but be ever apart. And we must wait. Our day would come, and we must press forward until it did, but we could not rush its fulfillment before God's time.

In the meantime, I lived in a world of dichotomies. My mother insisted I be well educated. Until I left the third grade, she drove me to school every day rather than letting me make the ten-minute walk. She wanted us to have the knowledge offered in my white school but did not trust that her children were safe walking to that white school. At the same time that she pushed me to learn everything my teachers had to teach, she also made sure we knew about Dred Scott and *Plessy v. Ferguson* and *Brown v. Board of Education* and volumes of other information my white teachers would never help me to know. We were in white society but not of white society. We worked within a system that we knew did not work for us. We grew strong and proud and knowledgeable knowing that the entire process made us even more the aliens in the world in which we lived.

Time worked in our favor, though. By 1970, the whites we knew got used to us. They realized we weren't there to destroy their neighborhood—or their lives! The violent acts went away. I made friends. People started to trust us and we learned we could trust them. I'm happy to say there were no more eggings or toilet paperings or reports of burnt crosses after 1971.

We were grateful as a family but still my parents worked to make us the exceptional black people they envisioned. In addition to the breakfast lessons intended to teach us our heritage, Mom enrolled us in a Jack and Jill group. This was a program for African American children to help them understand both their people's past and their worth. It was somewhat like Boy Scouts or Girl Scouts. We would gather on a Saturday afternoon in a family home and, in addition to lessons taught by the parents, there were often black doctors or policemen who would come and talk to us. They would tell us how to rise in society and about what kind of people we should be to succeed. The groups only met once a month but I remember to this day the sense of heritage, the righteous pride, and even the practical wisdom those Jack and Jill sessions embedded in me.

I understood from my earliest days that my parents were preparing me for a future of leadership. I may have been young but I realized that no other kid I knew was eating breakfast while their mother read *Uncle Tom's Cabin or Narrative of the Life of Frederick Douglass, an American Slave* or *Up From Slavery* by Booker T. Washington. I may have whined and staged small revolts from time to time but secretly I was glad for it. I had accepted my parents' insistence that destiny awaited and that I must be prepared for it.

CHAPTER 2

TAKING THE
TORCH IN HAND

P arents can prepare a child but they cannot force him to walk in the ways of his people. They can teach heritage, explain tactics, shape character, and do everything in their power to ignite destiny in the souls of their young. There must come that time, though, when the young take their destiny in hand. They must grasp the torch handed down, and make it their own by how they live and how they stand for their people.

This began for me when I first stepped into high school. I attended Shawnee Mission South, a school where there were only a handful of black students. When I look back upon those years, it is interesting that the only racist incidents that occurred were almost accidental, pretty much unintended. Nevertheless, the sense of self and purpose my parents had embedded in me helped me take a stand that brought change in each situation. Those episodes also sealed something in my soul, something lasting about being a black man in a sometimes unforgiving white world.

When I joined the football team at my new high school, the coach made it clear that he would only tolerate short hair. There would be no hair hanging from the back of helmets and no hair below the ears. Well, I was the only black kid on the team and I had an Afro at the time. And it was fine, let me tell you! It did not "hang" out of the helmet, it "puffed" out of the helmet. Now, the reason long hair was prohibited was that the coaches felt there needed to be a distinction between the way men and women were groomed. Thus, they were not going to have any young men sporting feminine hairstyles. I appealed: no one would ever confuse my "fro" as being feminine, but the coaches stood firm—"No cut, no play." I relented, but rather than let me go home and get an Afro-friendly haircut, the coaches got scissors used for cutting papier-mâché and started hacking away on my hair. There I sat, with other players looking on, tears streaming down my cheeks, while my Afro was destroyed.

When I got home and my father saw my head, he lost it. He immediately got on the phone, let the principal know everything on his mind, and then said the school should stand by to hear from his lawyers. No one thought he was bluffing. My father was all I wanted to be and at moments like this he stood tall and showed me what a heroic black man looks like.

When I arrived for football practice the next day, the situation had definitely changed. The coaches were all apologetic and gave me what can only be described as the royal treatment. Clearly, the higher ups in the school system had made some phone calls of their own. From that day forward, I had a great experience on that team. I also learned an important lesson: hair grows!

There was another incident from that time that was significant not only for what happened but for the reputation it earned me. It occurred when our school hosted a pep rally in support of the football team. Each player was represented by a cheerleader dressed up to look like them. Unfortunately, the cheerleader dressed up to look like me was in blackface.

Now, a great many non-blacks have a hard time understanding why blackface is such an insult to blacks. The simple explanation is that blackface has long been a way white minstrel shows and performers mimicked the most derogatory stereotypes of blacks. A white performer would put on blackface and then act as dumb as possible. They would prance around like someone afraid of their own shadow or like a mindless "Stepin Fetchit," the character played by the American comedian Lincoln Perry. It was all designed to put down a race and to show them as inferior, servile idiots worthy of ridicule and mistreatment.

Of course this is offensive to black folks! To understand this another way, suppose the people group being derided with something like blackface wasn't African Americans but all elderly people. Suppose it was all people in a wheelchair. I know it is hard to allow these images to form in our minds, but you see the point. We wouldn't hesitate to stop parodies of these groups, but we've simply grown used to people showing up at parties and on camera in blackface. Well, it has to stop, and I certainly knew it back then when I saw myself represented at that pep rally by a white girl in blackface.

It was at that moment that everything I had seen modeled by my parents rose up in me. The history lessons before school. The Jack and Jill meetings. The swimming pool. Immediately after that pep rally I made my way to the vice principal's office and announced that I was going to publicly make a stand at the school because of what had happened. I'll grant you I wasn't very articulate, but I was incensed and everyone in that office knew it. I told him what I had come to say. I said that representing me in blackface was wrong. I told him that no student should be treated that way. I said people at the school had to understand what blackface meant to blacks and to me personally.

To his credit, that VP told me he agreed and that such an episode would never happen again. Then, he called my parents and everyone else involved. The next day, people came up and apologized to me. They were sincere, too. More importantly, it never happened again.

Perhaps the most important thing to come out of this moment in my life, other than blackface ending at that school, was the way people saw me. The white students around me began to understand that I wasn't just a body with black skin, but I was a kid who belonged to something bigger than himself. I was part of a people. A people who had a past. It was a past that ennobled us but also left us with some sensitivities and with ways of looking at the world that often made us different from the non-blacks around us. Frankly, what I saw in the eyes of my white friends was a new level of respect, a new appreciation, perhaps, for what it meant to be black. Because of this, I'm grateful to this day for my parent's investment in me and the way it moved me to take a stand.

The reputation that I acquired through that situation followed me to a new school within the district. Because of an administrative decision to partition some of the area schools, I ended up going to a new high school. When I got there, I realized that news of what had happened at my former school had arrived ahead of me. You might think this led to some resentment. It didn't. Teachers spoke to me with a heightened level of respect. The other students would still talk smack and have fun with me but you could tell that they regarded me as someone who "represented," as we say today, someone who brought the beauty of being black—past and present—with them. It was all an early lesson for me in what it meant to stand up for who I am.

My life changed dramatically in the years after I graduated from high school. I had the opportunity to play football at Bethany College, which was two hundred miles from Kansas City in Lindsborg, Kansas. Now, Lindsborg, Kansas, is also known as "Little Sweden," and, baby, let me tell you, it is *white!* Not a black person lived in the town. Still, the people were nothing but kind and gracious. Though I was one of only 32 blacks out of 1,100 students at Bethany, there was never an embarrassing or offensive incident. I hung out mainly with my black friends and tried to do my best as a student and an athlete.

In my third year of college, I transferred to Indiana University. I'd like to tell you that I had some grand and important purpose for transferring to IU, but the truth is I had fallen for a girl and wanted to marry her. Thankfully, God works through such human impulses. He was certainly working in my life at the time, though I have to confess that I was about as far from him as I had ever been.

My spiritual life had been a bit of a winding road up until then. I had given my life to Jesus in Mrs. Robinson's living room when I was seven, as I've said. I also made a fresh commitment to God at fourteen while at a Fellowship Of Christian Athletes Conference, and had received a new enduement of power from the Holy Spirit at sixteen while at Full Faith Church Of Love in Kansas City, Missouri.

Around 1967-68, my family began attending Leawood Baptist Church, which was one of the most prestigious churches in the area. Even luminaries like Lamar Hunt, the famous businessman and sports entrepreneur, attended there. I can still remember our first days visiting that prominent and very white church. All eyes were on us. No one said anything but it was, let me tell you, very uncomfortable. Still, the longer we stayed, the better it got. People warmed up to us and, in time, we became part of that spiritual family. I grew to enjoy it.

In those days I did all the things a Baptist youth does. I went to Bible studies, attended "huddle groups," and got involved in the Fellowship of Christian Athletes. I spent summer months at youth camps. Leawood Baptist was huge and had a world of activities to offer. They really cared for my family and challenged me about Jesus. Even though we occasionally visited our former inner-city church home, Pleasant Green Baptist Church, there's no question that our lives at that time centered around Leawood Baptist. It shaped us in powerful ways. Still, by the time I got to Indiana University, I was definitely not living for Jesus and I knew it. I was about me, my desires, and my plans for the future.

That started to change one day when I was walking across campus. Suddenly, a young man stopped me and demanded, "Hey! You a Christian?" It was a shock. I said, "Me?" He said yes and repeated the question. I responded with my pride injured, "Well, it depends on your definition of Christian." I guess I assumed that if this guy was stopping people on campus to preach to them then he probably didn't have the biblical base to back it up. Man, was I wrong. This guy did! By the time Randy Young was through telling me what a true Christian was, I realized I wasn't close to living like one. I was spiritually dull and the more this guy talked to me the duller I felt.

I suppose he could tell that, though I was uncertain, I was open, because he invited me to a meeting where a professional football player was scheduled to tell his story. I could have blown it off, but I was interested. Clearly, God was working through that moment. I agreed to see him at the meeting.

The man who was scheduled to speak was named James Jones. He had been drafted by the Dallas Cowboys and had played college football at Mississippi State. The guy who stopped me on campus was also from Mississippi State. I had to wonder why in the world all these southern boys were hanging around Indiana University. I asked the guy about this and he said that he was on an outreach during his spring break from college. This answer really blew me away. That a guy would give up his spring break to preach to people he didn't even know really impressed me. I told him, "Dude, I've never met a Christian like you."

Clearly, the Holy Spirit was drawing me, and it is pretty amazing the obstacles he can work through. When I arrived for the seminar, I learned that James Jones had a family emergency. Another man, Nick Papas, was going to speak in his place. Before we got to his talk, though, there was worship. Believe me, I had never seen anything like it! The guy leading songs was clearly a lover of country music. He was from southern Indiana and it showed. Lots of guitar, lots of twang, lots of nasal. In response, though, the people were raising their hands and shouting—perhaps it was singing—at the top of their voices. I started looking for a way to leave. In near panic, I realized I couldn't get out.

There were only twenty-five people there, so I really felt exposed. That feeling didn't leave me when Nick Papas started to preach. He spoke for over an hour. Now, I had never heard an hour-long sermon in my life. Papas hit hard and took no prisoners. He ended his message by asking, "If Jesus were to walk through that door right now, how many of you would go with him?" Everyone raised their hand. I tried to join them but couldn't. I mean, I literally could not raise my hand. God wouldn't let me. Nick Papas noticed. Oh man, did he notice! He looked at me with ferocity and asked, "How come you wouldn't go?" I was speechless. I said nothing. He asked, "Is it pride?" I squeaked out, "Yes."

Papas was nothing if not bold. "Stand up and repent right now!" I stood. The guy next to me had to do the same. Apparently he was as evil as I was. Nick led us in a prayer. Then, gratefully, it was all over. Everyone "gave the Lord a handclap" and went home.

Before I could leave the building, the pastor of the church, a man named Mitch Smith, approached me and the guy who had stood up with me. He said, "I'm so sorry. That's not how ministry should be done." I remember thinking, "That's big. That's really big of this man." Then he looked at me and said, "Come back on Monday. I want to do a Bible study with you." Surprisingly, I agreed.

When I was meeting with Pastor Smith, one of the most astounding moments of my life occurred. He was sharing the Bible with me when he suddenly turned to me and said, "Let me ask you a question. Do you have one leg shorter than the other?"

Now, the fact was, I did—and there was no way that this man could have known it. I did the triple jump on the school's track team and the percussion of that sport had started causing me back troubles. X-rays showed that I had a crooked spine and one leg shorter than the other. The truth is that most people do have one leg shorter than the other and that it causes them troubles even though they may not know the source. Mine was pretty acute. So, I told the pastor, "Yes."

He told me to sit down so he could pray for me. Now, growing up Baptist, I thought that meant he was going to pray later! When I told him this, he said, "No, no, I want to pray for you now." He had me sit in a chair with the small of my back all the way against the back of the chair. Then he started to pray. I distinctly remember that he was pressing against my legs, rather than pulling them forward. This is important, because if he wanted to fake a result, he would have pulled my short leg forward. Instead, he pushed me back. It was almost as though he wanted to make it harder on God. He wanted real results, not some imagined or manipulated experience.

He had only prayed for about forty-five seconds when I felt a distinct popping in my knee and my hip. It was so startling that I gave out a loud, "Ow!" Then I stood. It is the absolute truth that my legs were even. It felt good! In fact, I felt better than I had in a long time. At the pastor's suggestion, I lifted my hands like a man being arrested to praise God and express my joy.

Now you have to remember that I was a Baptist. We loved Jesus and delighted in the Bible, but it was pretty much accepted that the day of miracles had long ago passed away. God loved people. God saved people. God ruled the world. But healings? That was more associated with Pentecostals than with Baptists, and we didn't really believe in it anyway.

Well, when a miracle happens, all reasoning against it goes away. All opposition crumbles in a second. I thanked that pastor and ran a quarter of a mile home. Then, I called my mom and told her what had happened. God had done a miracle! For me! I hardly let her get a word in edgewise and I'm sure I freaked her out.

From that day forward, I was on fire. I had to share my new love for God and the gratitude I felt for him healing me. I started preaching to everyone I knew and many I didn't on that campus—between classes, before classes, at lunch, and even on the grassy areas between the school's buildings. No one had to ask me, I just dove in. Now, I'm sure I offended people. Frankly, I didn't know what I was doing. I was just a man filled with excitement about what God had done. Over time, I gentled up and learned some finesse in talking to people about spiritual things, but at that time I was filled with the zeal of the convert.

I do recall having a thought that grew into something important in my life. I remember thinking, "Hey, Brett. You know, there aren't a lot of people doing what you're doing. So, what's going on inside of you that is different? Other folks, even Christian folks, don't necessarily have the drive that you do. What does that mean for your life?"

While these questions stirred in my soul, I kept moving. That meeting with Pastor Smith and the healing of my legs occurred in Spring of 1981. I finished my junior year and then attended some courses that summer to help me get better at preaching and talking about spiritual things. That fall, I got back to preaching in the open air. I was no less excited than I had been, but now I had a little bit of knowledge about how to hook people and draw them to the Lord.

I got good at using intellectual bait. I would shout out to a crowd of people, "Does anybody believe there are absolutes?" Inevitably, someone would stop and insist, "No, there are no absolutes!" Then I would answer, "Really? Are you absolutely sure? Because you just made an absolute statement that contradicts your assertion when you said 'there are no absolutes'. In fact, by making your statement, you have confirmed that your inner man, who knows that there must be absolutes, is fighting with your intellect. The bridge between truth and your conclusions has broken down. The contradiction between you and your own opinion needs resolve." I would then start preaching about the one who was qualified to issue absolutes—the living God. A crowd would always start to form and that's when I would head into offering people a chance to respond to the gospel.

I admit that this was an odd way to start out in ministry. Yet this was my boot camp, where I cut my teeth in preaching the gospel. By December of 1981, those questions that had been swirling around in my mind resolved themselves. I knew I was called to go into the ministry.

As happens in the lives of many people who answer the call of God, my decision to go into the ministry created tensions in my family. It had always been my dad's hope that I would follow him into dentistry. I had already somewhat disappointed him by wanting to be a veterinarian. I had always loved animals and cared about their well-being. For one year, I corresponded with the National Wildlife Federation concerning their initiative to save endangered wild horses. I even spent a week interning with a veterinarian in my neighborhood. Unfortunately, when the time came, I couldn't get into veterinary school. I had been a good student at Bethany and pulled a 3.5 grade point average (GPA), but when I got to Indiana, my busyness in ministry got in the way of my studies and I only earned a 2.7 GPA. You had to have a 3.9 for veterinary school.

Trying to find my way, I applied to my father's school, Meharry Medical College in Nashville. After being accepted into what would be the graduating class of '85, I resigned my seat in July of 1982 and set out to raise funds in order to serve God as an occupational minister, performing my service on the campus of Howard University in Washington, DC.

My father was not happy. As a proud, self-sufficient man himself, he was embarrassed in front of all his fellow alums that his son rejected his alma mater. He was also embarrassed that I would dare to ask people for money so I could minister.

There is a back story here you need to know. You see, my parents raised me not to ask for anything. I was trained to be self-reliant and dependent on no one. Even when I visited someone's house, I was not supposed to ask for a drink of water. It is simply what was expected of me. In my parents' home, there was definitely a culture resistant to asking for anything, which means there was resistance to any form of fundraising or asking for financial support.

So I became an embarrassment to my father, my mother, and nearly everyone we knew. I had stuck a knife in my father's heart with the life I had chosen. He thought I had brought shame on the family and said as much. It did not help that my mother and father had divorced and later my mother married a minister. My father thought I wanted to be more like my stepfather than like him, and so a great wall arose between us. It nearly ended our relationship. It got to the point that all we could peacefully talk about was how the Kansas City Chiefs or the Royals were doing. It was tragic and painful.

And it got worse. That December I returned home for Christmas and learned that my brother had woefully underperformed in his first semester as a freshman at TCU. My father started talking about what disappointments his boys were. At dinner one night, he turned to my brother and said, "See him?" He gestured toward me. "He's nothing. He will always be nothing. Don't you ever come home like him!"

My father probably not only thought I was wasting my talents in ministry, but that perhaps I was choosing an easy, lazy lifestyle. He had seen excesses among some ministers before and was disgusted by it. In my case, he couldn't have been further from the truth. The reality is that at that time I was not only living lean but living—once again—in the difficult chasm between two worlds.

You see, I was ministering at Howard University (though not as an employee of the institution), one of the great HBCUs in the United States. The culture at Howard was a culture I understood and loved. Parents sent their children to Howard to be dyed-in-the-wool black people, to be part of a black movement. They wanted immersion in black culture—and they got it. African American history wasn't just an elective. It was central to academic life. It was at the heart of what the school was about. It was black culture without dilution, a complete devotion to preserving who we are while nurturing all we hoped to be as a black people.

So I was serving on that campus and naturally feeling a part of it. On Sundays, though, I was a minister in the largely white church which I had helped to plant. The church was founded and led by a fine man, Mark Caulk. He strummed his guitar with a country flair as he led worship. He was a gifted minister who was an exemplary shepherd to the flock of God. A real lover of people, his sacrificial care was abundant, but his experience in relating to "us" was limited. Making the difficulty all the greater, it was my job to convince students from Howard to attend my culturally and predominately white church. It wasn't easy but I did see some success. We never had more than 180 people and of that number about 35 were black. And we were proud of that ratio. This was at a time when Dr. King had made famous a saying that Sunday morning was the most segregated time in American life. We were beating the average and we were proud of it.

The truth was, though, that most of the black kids were staying there because I encouraged them to. I told them it was important to break down barriers. I believed this with all my heart, but I knew it was hard for them. When I would go on campus to do a Bible study, I would sometimes hear the black students from our church mimicking the worship style they heard on Sundays. They would sing through their nose at the top of their voices and perfectly capture the accent of our worship. Then they'd break out in great peals of laughter. When they saw me approaching, though, they would suddenly stop. I would always tell them not to worry. "Listen, I get it. I get it." Still, I told them, I was proud of them for stepping over ethnic lines that were like prison walls for most people in the rest of the country.

I lived between these two worlds—between the black and the white, between Howard University and my white church—for the next nine years. It was a time of learning, stretching, and growing up in God. It was also an extremely busy time. I did just about everything at that church except preach on Sundays. I set up the equipment for our services. I was the evangelism trainer. I was chaplain for the Howard football team. I did student ministry, and anything else I was asked to do. No complaint. It was a privilege to serve. It was a God-ordained season and I knew it. The Lord often trains his servants on the frontlines and in the heat of duty. I'm grateful he put me in that school of the Holy Spirit all those years. Still, it all meant living on the stretch for God.

Then it happened. In 1991, the pastor announced that it was time for a change. The ministry of which the church had been part, a movement called Maranatha, had dissolved in 1989. The collateral effect among the local churches was significant. After eighteen months, the senior pastor of our congregation felt that his time leading our church had come to an end. He came to me and asked me if I would step in. He said the church would only survive if I took the helm.

It was not an easy decision for me. I had other opportunities. I had been working on my theology degree at Chesapeake Theological Seminary and this brought me into contact with other ministers and churches who expressed an interest in me working with them. I had been living on the financial ragged edge for quite a while. I was providing for my wife and our two boys under three years of age while caring for my terminally ill father. The idea of staying at a church of about seventy people didn't have as much allure as the opportunities that shone brightly on the horizon.

Still, I knew better than to make decisions based on ambition or money. I also knew better than to make decisions based on need or opportunity alone. If I had learned anything during those nine years in the school of the Holy Spirit, it was that you seek God about all things and make decisions based on his guidance alone. This is what I did—and God said to stay.

So in May of 1991, I took the lead of our little church. I asked the congregation to be patient with me. In fact, I remember saying it this way: "Pastor Mark left some big shoes to fill. There is no way that I can be him. Please just give me a little time to grow up, to go to the store, and to get my own pair of new shoes. Give me three months to win your confidence in my leadership." At the end of that three months, we were down seventeen people. Yes, my skill set had grown the church from seventy people to fifty-three! I was on my way—down!

Still, I hung in. After one year, I had the same number of people. Some of those fifty-three were brand new, which meant some of the original fifty-three found greener pastures. I was battling discouragement, but I was determined not to quit as the Lord was proving himself reliable. Two things happened. First, God surrounded me with some amazing men, heroes of mine who are still in my life today. These men were accomplished in their own fields—some of them even NFL stars—but they stood with me, built with me, and kept me strong in those challenging days.

The second thing that happened is that I went looking for a movement to which I could belong. Our church was unattached to any network of churches or denomination at that time and I knew that wasn't the way it should be. I went in search of a home for my people. And I found one. From the relational connections of the Maranatha movement, a new network called MorningStar arose. I attended one of their conferences in Los Angeles to dig deeper into what I knew about them. I had already known the leaders for over a decade. They were white but they didn't want to build a white movement and they were deeply devoted to college ministry and church planting. I remember thinking that I had already been walking with these guys for so many years that I should just stick with my history. Within a year, I joined. Finally, I had a people to build with, a people who shared my vision. Finally, I had comrades with whom I could build something bigger than my own local house.

The meaning of my journey was starting to take shape. My constant living between two worlds, disappointing my parents, leaving the way they had chosen for me, and living as a radical for God—all of it was finally beginning to coalesce into who I was becoming and what I was helping to lead in the early 1990s.

Here is the heart of it all. Once I began realizing that pastoring was my life's work, that it was not something I had stumbled into but something God had fashioned me for, I found a single prayer almost shouting itself from my inner being. It was this: "Lord, if you are going to give me opportunity to pastor a church, please make it look more like heaven than like me."

It was a prayer inspired by what I had read in scripture about what heaven is like. We are told in Revelation 7:9, for example, about the scene that surrounds God's throne. The apostle John writes, "After this I looked, and there before me was a great multitude that no one could count, from every nation, tribe, people and language, standing before the throne and before the Lamb."

Our great God, who can enthrone himself anywhere he chooses, has decided to rule in heaven in the midst of people from every kind of nation, from all the different tribes, and of every language group. This is his delight. This is what he has created. This is what he has redeemed through his son Jesus and has chosen as the setting for his rule over the universe.

I read these words and I was changed by them. How could I ever be satisfied with a one color, one language, one nation, one tribe church when my Heavenly Father delighted to enthrone himself in the splendor of all them? How could I live a Great Commission that commanded me to "make disciples of all nations" but be satisfied being part of a local church comprised of just one type of people? Frankly, to settle for the *one* when I knew we Christians were called to disciple the *many* seemed almost a sin. Thus my prayer: "Lord, if you are going to give me opportunity to pastor a church, please make it look more like heaven than like me."

This vision and this prayer came with a holy dissatisfaction. I was not critical of other churches but I could not be satisfied with anything less than an earthly, local church that looked like what the Bible describes of heaven. It has become my life's work. It has become my passion. It has brought me into conflict with the culture around me and even, at times, with the church world itself. It has meant sleepless nights and mystified friends and a sometimes slower pace than might have been possible for an easier purpose. Still, I know it is what I am made to do, made to build, and made to stand for.

You can understand, then, why I cannot remain silent while standing as I am today, amidst the racial chaos and turbulence of 2020. I am not just a man who lives between the white world and the black. I am also a man who lives between a clear-eyed understanding of current reality and the heavenly vision of what God intends. I am, like so many others, caught in the crush between the two. It makes what is going on around me in this generation all the more painful, all the most desperate, all the more an urgent moment I must address with every resource at my command.

CHAPTER 3

THE PRESS OF THE PAST UPON US

H istory is far more than a cold recitation of facts. It is the experience of a people. It is the annals of the forces that have made them what they are. In filmmaker Ken Burns's wise phrase, history is the "emotional architecture" of the human experience. In this view, then, it should not be difficult to understand that the "emotional architecture" of the black experience in America is far different from that of any other people.

Our story began a year before the *Mayflower* landed at Plymouth. In aid of a failing Jamestown Colony huddled on the shores of the New World, an English privateer offloaded twenty slaves. These Africans were acquired during a raid on a Spanish vessel making for Vera Cruz, a city in what is now Mexico. When slaves with names like Isabella,

Pedro, and Antoney first stepped upon the soil of Virginia in 1619, black America began.[1]

This was the New World's first foray into a holocaust that had started with Muslim Arabs in the 700s and then exploded with the Portuguese in 1442. Before it was done, more than forty million African souls would be uprooted and chained to dreams of arrogant power.

Men lied to themselves to content their souls that there was something God-ordained about slavery. Blacks were heathen, after all, and so enslaving them might lead to their conversion. Then, they could be freed. In time, though, this deceit collapsed under the weight of greed. A 1667 Virginia law removed all doubt: "The conferring of baptisme doth not alter the condition of the person as to his bondage or freedom."[2]

The slave trade thus became accepted for just what it was—a vile trade in human bodies. Men knew of the suffocating, coffin-like conditions on the slave ships of the Middle Passage and did nothing. They also knew that so many black bodies were shoved overboard during these voyages, made useless to their owners by death or madness, that sharks learned to follow the ships departing the coast of Africa for the New World. They knew of the markets and the humiliating inspections and the whippings. They knew of the shattered families, of the rapes, and of the working of bodies until they could work no more.

They knew. And they excused. And they justified. And they wrapped it all in the cloth of Christianity and a vision of white rule on earth.

---

1 Carl Bridenbaugh, *Jamestown, 1544-1699* (New York: Oxford University Press, 1980), p. 51.

2 Carl Bridenbaugh, *Jamestown, 1544-1699*, p. 46

Slavery has been called "America's original sin." It is true. Slavery pitted North against South in colonial America and forced the compromises and fictions that deformed the heart of the nation.

Bitter as the truth is, we must recount the past as it was. While blacks were enslaved and denied the basic rights of human beings in British America, they fought to make this land what it would be. To echo the famous words, "We were there."

We were there in 1676, when blacks fought alongside whites in Bacon's Rebellion, an armed protest to force government back into its proper confines.

We were there in Boston in 1770 when a skirmish that became known as the Boston Massacre led to the death of a black sailor named Crispus Attucks. He was the first American martyr in the revolutionary cause.

We were there at Lexington and Concord, where black men like Prince Easterbrooks fought and bled. We were also there at Bunker Hill, where Barzillai Lew served, just as he would serve in the Continental Army for another seven years.

We were there again and again and again. We crossed the Delaware with Washington and suffered with him at Valley Forge. We captured British generals, worked secretly behind enemy lines, and served in battle after battle with distinction. There were five thousand of us who fought in the American cause and many of us were celebrated. A black solider named Salem Poor is remembered in a memorial at Cambridge, Massachusetts, as a man who "behaved like an experienced officer, as well as an excellent soldier."[3] Even the enemy honored the black soldiers

---

3 Jeffrey C. Stewart, *1001 Things Everyone Should Know About African American History* (New York: Doubleday, 1996), p. 185.

among the American forces. A Hessian officer reported to his superiors, "no regiment is to be seen in which there are not Negroes in abundance, and among them there are able bodied, strong and brave fellows"[4]

We were there.

It didn't seem to matter, though, because when Thomas Jefferson declared his "self-evident truth" to the world that "all men are created equal," he and his generation did not mean blacks. This became painfully obvious when the members of the Constitutional Convention in 1787 concluded that a black man counted as only three-fifths of a human being in determining representation.

Now, I admire the founding fathers. I'm grateful for what they gave us, though I certainly think that they were flawed and that those who were opposed to slavery did not oppose it hard enough.

Still, if you are ever going to understand the controversy black Americans have with America today, you must understand that the great Constitution that is the basis for our society said that my ancestors were only three-fifths of a human being. I fully understand that this designation, known as the Three-fifths Compromise, was conceived as a concession that attempted to bring equity between the North and South with respect to how each should be represented in the House of Representatives. Still, this formal designation of our less-than-fully-human status is degrading. This means that my people ranked just above a cow to those who founded our country.

Now, that generation knew that blacks were human beings. Think about it. Whites of that time fought alongside blacks. Many entrusted their children to blacks. In fact, African Americans helped or led in

---

4 Lerone Bennett Jr., *Before the Mayflower: A History of Black America* (New York: Penguin Books, 1993), p. 31.

nearly every endeavor of the new nation. No one seriously believed that blacks were not human. No one. Despite this, the founding generation built into its laws the idea that blacks should not be counted as complete human beings.

Looking back upon that time, we can tell that American society was wrestling with its conscience. The Northwest Ordinance of 1787 forbade slavery in the new territories that were becoming states. Tennessee chose to ignore this law, and the floodgates opened. In 1808, Congress passed a law that forbade the importation of slaves into the country. It, too, was ignored everywhere.

The founding message was clear. Blacks are damaged creatures. They are less. Their very nature is inferior. And this belief—signaled by practice if not by doctrine—flowed from generation, to generation, to generation, for two centuries afterward.

Here is my conclusion. This nation wasn't made for me. The Constitution wasn't made for me. They were made *on* me—and on the backs of people like me.

Still, black Americans tried to find loopholes in the law to get them out of their chains. One of the most dramatic was the Supreme Court's famous Dred Scott decision in 1857. Dred Scott was a slave whose master had taken him to live in Illinois and the Wisconsin Territory, both of which were "free" territories. The laws stated that slaveholders surrendered their rights to their slaves if they dwelled in such free regions for an extended time. Scott's owner lived there for four years. So Scott sued for his freedom.

The case ultimately became about whether an African American could claim citizenship in the United States. The court's majority opinion, written by Chief Justice Roger Taney, concluded that blacks had "no rights which the white man was bound to respect; and that the negro might justly and lawfully be reduced to slavery for his benefit."[5] Let those words burn into your memory: "no rights which the white man was bound to respect." They echo down through the years, as they should.

Given such views, it is no wonder that our nation was tortured by its original sin of slavery again and gain. We were forced to fight a grinding, ghastly war over this sin. We call it the Civil War but it was the most un-civil of our history. It cost us 700,000 lives and a legacy of bitterness that continues today. We should remember, and every school child should know, that while our nation rent itself asunder over this issue of black liberty, England eradicated slavery with the stroke of a pen in the early 1830s. This was because of the work of William Wilberforce and his team of reforming evangelicals.

The American who came closest to this same sense of God's will in the matter of slavery was Abraham Lincoln. In his First Inaugural Address, given in 1861, he spoke to the Southern states as the per-petrators and said they were the ones in whose hands the matter of peace rested. After four years of bloodletting, though, he had come to a different view. In his Second Inaugural Address, given a few months before his death, he spoke of his conclusion that God had visited the war on the nation because of its treatment of blacks. It is a tragedy that the whole country could not have come to the same conclusion before so many lives were ground up on battlefields and so much heartache spilled out into the land.

There is another fact that every American schoolchild should know. It is that when Lincoln signed the Emancipation Proclamation

---

5 Dred Scott v. Standford, 60 U.S. at 407 (1857), https://supreme.justia.com/cases/federal/us/60/393/

freeing the slaves in 1863, he did so because of a covenant he had made with God. We have witnesses to this fact and it is undeniable. At the cabinet meeting in which Lincoln announced his decision, Salmon Chase, the secretary of the treasury, was in attendance and recorded Lincoln's words in his diary. Here is the relevant portion:

> Gentlemen, I have, as you are aware, thought a great deal about the relation of this war to Slavery; and you all remember that, several weeks ago, I read to you an Order I had prepared on this subject, which, on account of objections made by some of you, was not issued. Ever since then, my mind has been much occupied with this subject, and I have thought all along that the time for acting on it might very probably come. I think the time has come now. I wish it were a better time. I wish that we were in a better condition. The action of the army against the rebels has not been quite what I should have liked. But they have been driven out of Maryland, and Pennsylvania is no longer in danger of invasion. When the rebel army was at Frederick, I determined, as soon as it should be driven out of Maryland, to issue a Proclamation of Emancipation such as I thought most likely to be useful. I said nothing to any one; *but I made the promise to myself, and (hesitating a little)—to my Maker. The rebel army is now driven out, and I am going to fulfill that promise.*[6]

Gideon Welles, secretary of the navy, was also at this meeting and, like Chase, wrote of it in his diary:

---

6 David Donald, *Inside Lincoln's Cabinet: The Civil War Diaries of Salmon P. Chase* (New York: Longmans, Green & Co., 1954), 149–150. Emphasis mine.

In the course of the discussion on this paper, which was long, earnest, and on the general principle involved, harmonious, *he remarked that he had made a vow, a covenant, that if God gave us the victory in the approaching battle he would consider it an indication of Divine will, and that it was his duty to move forward in the cause of emancipation.* It might be thought strange, he said, that he had in this way submitted the disposal of matters when the way was not clear to his mind what he should do. God had decided this question in favor of the slaves. He was satisfied it was right, was confirmed and strengthened in his action by the vow and the results.[7]

So at least some of our leaders understood that the nation was on the wrong side of both God and justice in this matter of slavery. Lincoln and others were trying to set us right. Still, even when the war was done and Lincoln was in the grave, the nation continued to tear itself apart over this same issue.

I should pause here and note that I have referred several times to black people prior to the Civil War as African Americans. I've done this because it is a standard way to refer to early generations of blacks in America, but it wasn't true. We weren't Americans. We weren't allowed to be. Even after the Civil War, we were denied the full rights of citizens. It would take the Thirteenth Amendment to the Constitution in 1865 before a black man or woman could legally be called African American, and at least another hundred years before the deserved respect that should have come with that designation would be earned.

---

7 John T. Morse, Jr., ed., *Diary of Gideon Welles: Secretary of the Navy Under Lincoln and Johnson,* 3 vols. (Boston: Houghton Mifflin, 1911), 1:142–143. Emphasis mine.

Still, we began well in the wake of the war. Inspired by the intent of the Emancipation Proclamation, our country abolished slavery in the Thirteenth Amendment to its Constitution. It then undid the damage of the Dred Scott decision in the Fourteenth Amendment which proclaimed, among other things, that ex-slaves were citizens of the United States. Soon after, it established in the Fifteenth Amendment to the Constitution that voting rights could not be kept from citizens based on "race, color, or previous condition of servitude."

It seemed for a while that a grand correction might be underway. It seemed that perhaps the nation was righting itself. Then came Reconstruction, a season of excess in which the North visited its vengeance on the South largely by using unsuspecting blacks as weapons. Hatred seethed and conspiracies were conceived. The Ku Klux Klan, a century of racism, and a legacy of Southern resentment resulted.

The evils of "Jim Crow" laws followed. As early as 1877, these laws operated in the South and some border states, institutionalizing the status of blacks as second-class citizens. The laws were petty and demeaning. A black hairdresser couldn't serve white women. Libraries had to have separate space for black readers to keep them from mixing with white readers. Blacks trying to travel on a bus had to use separate restrooms, buy their ticket at a separate ticket counter, and sit in separate waiting rooms from whites. And so it went. There were thousands of such laws. There were even rules about whether a white man could shake a black man's hand or whether a black man could demonstrate superior knowledge about a subject in the presence of a white man. It was tyranny by custom and legal code, and it undid all the good that was won by the Civil War and the laws that came in its aftermath.

Nor was this just Southern custom and oppression. In 1896, the US Supreme Court confirmed this treatment of blacks by ruling in <u>Plessy v. Ferguson</u> that racial segregation laws were constitutional. Facilities for blacks and whites could legally be separate as long as they were equal in quality and access. The reality was, though, that they seldom were. You've likely seen the same photos I have. Facilities for blacks were squalid and degrading. That was the point: to subjugate blacks once again by, as the King James Bible says, "framing mischief by a law."[8]

We Americans pride ourselves on the fact that in 1954 the Supreme Court ruled in <u>Brown v. Board of Education</u> that racial segregation of children in public schools was unconstitutional. I'm grateful for this ruling, but we often remember it for something it wasn't. The court didn't overturn the Plessy decision. It only made separate but equal illegal in education. Although the legal profession would progressively apply the ruling of <u>Brown vs. Board of Education</u> to other unlawful segregation statutes and practices, much of the mistreatment of blacks justified by the <u>Plessy v. Ferguson</u> "separate but equal" decision lived on.

Now perhaps you can better understand why my grandfather, a professor at Tuskegee and a bank president, refused to spend his money on the white side of town. Just picture it. When he went to the white side of town, he who had a PhD in from University of Pennsylvania would be addressed as "boy"—or worse. He could not allow his intelligence to show in white company. He dared not pay too much kind attention to a white woman, even in the most casual greeting. He could not initiate a handshake with a white man. He would always be addressed by his first name, while he was expected to address every white person as Mr. or Mrs.

So while all the laws and customs were designed to treat this accomplished man like a contagious leper, as though black skin was a sign of threatening evil, my grandfather was expected to spend his

---

8 Psalm 94:20, KJV

money on the white side of town and therefore enrich the very people who hated and oppressed him. My grandfather was not only a smart man, he was an economist. He knew what economic injustice looked like and he knew that if the black community was going to prosper it would need to keep black money in black hands. He was right, but it shouldn't have been necessary. Something better in America was possible. Hatred, bitterness, and bigotry kept it from being so.

As we entered the twentieth century then, despite our nation being a hostile place for us, we were there.

We were there with Theodore Roosevelt when he and the Rough Riders charged up San Juan Hill during the Spanish American War. We were there in World War I, some 350,000 strong, serving in support units as well as fighting on the frontlines. In fact, 171 African Americans were awarded the French Legion of Honor for their heroic service during that vicious war.

Tragically, we were also there along with the rest of the nation during the Spanish Flu epidemic of 1918. More than 675,000 Americans died of that flu, and nearly 100 million people worldwide. Yet African Americans died at a higher rate than whites, largely because they were denied essential medical care by "Whites Only" hospitals.

Soon after, we suffered with the rest of the nation during the Great Depression and, naturally, our suffering was deeper than it needed to be because we were black and being black in those days meant you could be denied the relief granted to other Americans. Nevertheless, we were among the crews that built the Hoover Dam, the Lincoln Tunnel, the Golden Gate Bridge, and dozens of the other epic projects of that era. Every time we were called upon, we were there, no matter the treatment our nation doled out to us.

That's why we were there in World War II. More than 125,000 of us served overseas. More than 708 of us never returned home. The American cemeteries in Europe and Asia are dotted with black graves. Once again, we were heroic in the fight. The Tuskegee Airmen made history not only as the first African American flying corps but also for their stunning successes in battle. Black warriors showed themselves able and brave in every contest of that great battle between tyranny and freedom.

It all should have been enough. We had proven ourselves, not only as warriors and laborers, but as devoted patriots and good citizens—and this in a nation that was not devoted to us. When President Truman started integrating the US military in 1948, with segregated black units outlawed by 1954, it was in recognition of the fact that we had shown ourselves worthy, that all forms of separation and denigration were undeserved, immoral, and, frankly, un-American.

Still, the abuses continued, as they had all along. Shortly after World War I—a war in which blacks had served so impressively—there came an episode now known today as the Tulsa Race Riot. It was a stunning moment of racist violence that still haunts our nation today.

There had seldom been a tragedy like it, and particularly so for the history that had come just before it. As the twentieth century dawned, many blacks had begun to flood into Oklahoma in hopes of building free and prosperous lives for themselves. Some of these had been slaves of the Native American tribes in the area. Others were fleeing racial oppression elsewhere in the United States. The word spread. Oklahoma promised a safe haven for African Americans.

In fact, between 1865 and 1920, African Americans started more than fifty townships in that state. Some blacks became quite prosperous too. One of these, O. W. Gurley, a wealthy landowner, purchased forty acres of land in Tulsa and called it Greenwood after a Mississippi town he admired. Gurley's dream was to create a thriving community that would be both a haven for beleaguered blacks and a symbol of black ingenuity nationwide—perhaps even worldwide.

Gurley's vision steadily became a reality and Greenwood was soon called "The Black Wall Street." Entrepreneurship was encouraged. Business loans were widely available. On Greenwood Avenue, there were luxury shops, restaurants, hotels, clothing stores, movie theaters, night clubs, and libraries. Greenwood had its own school system, post office, savings and loan bank, hospital, and bus and taxi services. The offices of doctors, lawyers, and dentists lined its elegant avenues. The Greenwood newspaper gave blacks news vital to their lives and also sought to educate readers about the rights and civil liberties black Americans ought to enjoy.

In short, Greenwood thrived. In fact, it became the envy of whites in Tulsa. The phrase "they don't deserve that" was often on the lips of Tulsa's white citizens and often in the articles of the city's white newspapers. The blacks of Greenwood knew this was dangerous. We should remember that during this time the Ku Klux Klan was on the rise in America, lynchings were proliferating around the country, and there had been widespread anti-black riots in American cities, particularly during the "Red Summer" of 1919.

This brings us to May 31, 1921. The scene is the Drexel Building. It was there that a nineteen-year-old black shoe shiner named Dick Rowland was accused of sexually assaulting a seventeen-year-old white elevator operator named Sarah Page. For blacks, this kind of accusation was nothing new. Black men are often accused of having an unnatural affinity for white women and the mere rumor of impropriety has led to riots and murder time and again in American history.

This was the spark that set Tulsa on fire. Upon hearing the accusation against Dick Rowland, a white crowd went to the courthouse to demand that the sheriff hand the man over to them. The sheriff, who was still investigating the charges, rightly refused. Then twenty-five black men, most of them World War I veterans, armed themselves and went to the courthouse to help the sheriff guard Rowland. Word spread that a lynching was about to occur, and so more armed black men descended on the courthouse. They were met there by 1,500 whites.

Clashes began. The pent up animosities of years spilled into the streets. Whites descended on Greenwood and began looting homes, burning down businesses, and shooting blacks at will. At this point, accounts get murky. Between 300 and 3,000 blacks were killed. Keep in mind that the district's population was 10,000 at the time. More than 1,500 homes were burned to the ground and over 600 black-owned businesses were bombed. Libraries, schools, and even hospitals were also torched.

It grew worse. Whites who owned airplanes took to the sky and began bombing Greenwood. Homemade turpentine balls were the weapon of choice. These set buildings on fire from the top down, killing those caught unaware in the floors below. Pilots also fired guns from their planes which, according to witnesses, circled for hours. Historians still debate whether the Greenwood section of Tulsa was the first American community to be bombed from the air, but most conclude there is no evidence to the contrary.

Though it was the whites who were rioting, the National Guard interned more than 6,000 African Americans at the Convention Hall and Fairgrounds, some for as long as eight days. Meanwhile, the city burned. Looting was rampant. The killing continued.

The riot continued through the night of May 31 and all the next day. When it was over, Black Wall Street was no more. Greenwood barely existed. A prosperous, vital, innovative community—one of the most commendable in the nation—ceased to exist.

In time, the devastating word reached the agonized blacks of Tulsa: insurance companies would not pay for the losses. It had been a riot. It was blamed on the blacks. They had brought it on themselves, it was said. Their losses were their own. The blacks of Tulsa have still not recovered what they lost, even to this day.

At the time, the story barely made the back pages of the *New York Times*. Since then, nearly the same has been true in American public school textbooks. Seldom is the riot ever mentioned. When it is, the tale is never fully told. Never, of course, is there a chapter titled something like "The White Riot of Tulsa." But that is indeed what happened. And American blacks remember.

They also remember an episode of American history that is perhaps an even greater evil, even more a knife to the soul of black Americans. It was called the Tuskegee Syphilis Experiment, and for sheer callous indifference to human suffering, only the ghastly, degrading experiments of Nazi doctors offer a parallel.

Beginning in 1932, the forerunner of our modern Department of Health and Human Services, the United States Public Health Service, began conducting experiments on black men who had syphilis. These experiments were cunningly conducted at Tuskegee Institute, later Tuskegee University, one of the premier black institutions in the country. It was all made to seem well-intentioned and a service to African Americans.

Had the more than 400 black men involved been given legitimate medical care, the whole affair would barely be worth mentioning. Yet they weren't. These African American men weren't even told they had syphilis. They were told they had "bad blood," a local term used to describe a variety of illnesses like anemia and fatigue. They were assured they would be treated and that no harm would come to them. Instead, they were given placebos so that researchers could study the devastations of syphilis in real time.

Researchers told their subjects the experiments would last for six months. They lasted for forty years. Even after penicillin had long been established as a cure for syphilis, which was no later than 1947, the subjects of the experiment were kept unaware of their condition, were denied the proven cure, and were treated like human laboratory animals without regard for their health or well-being.

Because we have the cure for syphilis today, we don't remember how dreaded and severe the disease could be. It could lead to blindness. It could cause a victim to lose his hearing, suffer heart disease, or go mad. It could cause a host of relatively minor ailments and then, of course, it could lead to death.

Men died in the Tuskegee Syphilis Experiment and unnecessarily. Because researchers did not tell the men their true condition, many of them infected their wives. We know that forty wives contracted the disease and there may have been more. We also know that at least nineteen children were born with congenital syphilis as a result of the horrors being carried out at Tuskegee.

These evils didn't end until 1972. Think about that: This barbarity actually continued until 1972. It was only then that one of the researchers, a man named Peter Buxtun—thank God for him—leaked the details of the experiment to the press. This not only horrified American society but also led to dramatic changes in the laws governing scientific experiments.

Yet here was the all-important meaning of this episode, certainly the meaning to black America. In a nation that had codified slavery into its founding documents—that had determined a black man to be only three-fifths of a human being and that still denied basic rights to black Americans—it somehow seemed consistent that 400 men over a forty-year period could be treated like lab rats. They had black skin. They were therefore less human than white men. They were owed no protections. Let them suffer and infect and die—all without knowing they might—so that others with lighter skin could live free of a dreaded disease.

Twenty-four years after the experiment ended, President Bill Clinton apologized for what his country had done to those 400 black men and their families in Tuskegee. Saying that the Tuskegee Syphilis Study was "deeply, profoundly, morally wrong," Clinton concluded:

To the survivors, to the wives and family members, the children and the grandchildren, I say what you know: No power on Earth can give you back the lives lost, the pain suffered, the years of internal torment and anguish. What was done cannot be undone. But we can end the silence. We can stop turning our heads away. We can look at you in the eye and finally say, on behalf of the American people: what the United States government did was shameful. And I am sorry.[9]

9 NPR: Remembering the Tuskegee Experiment, (http://www.npr.org/programs/morning/features/2002/jul/Tuskegee/)

President Clinton was right, and I'm grateful he said it. Yet the meaning of it all lives on in the memory of black America.

I'm aghast at the great wickedness of the Tuskegee Syphilis Experiment, yet I'm also grateful for the other good things that occurred for blacks during those same years. I'm grateful that President Eisenhower signed the Civil Rights Act of 1957, allowing prosecution of those who tried to prevent a man or a woman from voting, and also establishing a commission to fight voter fraud. I'm grateful for the Civil Rights Act of 1964, which guaranteed equal employment for all, limited use of voter literacy tests, and ordered federal authorities to ensure integrated public facilities. I can't be anything but grateful for the Voting Rights Act of 1965—which again sought to remove barriers to voting— and the Fair Housing Act of 1968. Thank God for it all.

Yet, grateful as I am, I do not look upon these acts as the deeds of a benevolent nation. No, I look upon them as the victories won by my black heroes. I know it took a woman named Rosa Parks riding a Montgomery, Alabama, bus in 1955 to win these rights. It took nine black students courageously attending classes at Central High School in Little Rock, Arkansas. It took students facing vicious mobs at lunch counters and the Freedom Riders storming the South in 1963 and a March on Washington that same year. It also took Bloody Sunday in Selma and the murder of Dr. Martin Luther King Jr. and the gunning down of Medgar Evers and a thousand other courageous and some- times tragic deeds to bring it all about.

Now again, I love my nation but I do not believe that we have arrived where we are because a benevolent white America changed its mind. I believe my people earned our way here. We claimed our place. We cried out to God, studied hard, gave our money, banded together, and risked our lives in hope of what Dr. King called "the promised land" of American justice and freedom. We achieved. We made our case. We have risen.

I have not recounted all this history merely to complain. Nor have I told these stories to portray black Americans as always noble and good. We are all flawed. We are all sinners. There are no perfect people in this world.

Yet I have given this overview of history to help non-blacks—and maybe some uninformed blacks too—understand the imprint of the past upon us. Our history not only sets us apart as a people but it also conditions us. It shapes how we think, gives us the lens through which we view the world. It has also fashioned our souls, so that we feel and respond and react differently from our friends of other skin colors and ethnicities.

This brings us to our present moment, to the urgencies of 2020 and the single event that has sparked so much trouble and led to such advances in a short time in our country. Let's talk about the killing of George Floyd.

Here are the facts. On the evening of May 25, 2020, George Floyd walked into the Cup Foods grocery store in Minneapolis, Minnesota, and bought a pack of cigarettes. Floyd had moved to Minneapolis from Houston two years before and was known as a "gentle giant" among friends. He was athletic, had been a football star at Yates High School in Houston, and had played in the 1992 high school championship.

It is true he had his troubles. After once losing his job, he grew desperate and committed armed robbery. He served time in prison and when he was released he decided to make a difference in the world. He spoke out against gun violence and helped create a basketball court ministry at a housing project in his neighborhood. He stayed close to his church family.

Moving to Minneapolis for a fresh start, he worked hard, often working two jobs at a time. People who knew him found him "always cheerful." He was known for dancing badly just to get people to laugh. His dream was to bring his six-year-old daughter from Houston and then marry his fiancée, Courteney Ross. She described George as "nothing but an angel that was sent to us on earth."

He had been a regular at Cup Foods. The store owner, Mike Abumayyaleh, told reporters that George was a welcome friendly face, a pleasant customer who never caused any trouble.

Unfortunately, Mr. Abumayyaleh was not in his store at 8:01 p.m. on May 25. Instead, a teenaged employee was. It was then that the 911 call was made from the store. Floyd had tried to purchase a pack of cigarettes with a twenty-dollar bill. The teenaged clerk thought the bill looked counterfeit. He did what he was trained to do. He asked Floyd to return the cigarettes. Floyd refused. The clerk called 911.

Officers arrived on the scene at 8:08. Floyd was then sitting in a parked car around the corner from the store. Officer Thomas Lane approached the parked car and drew his gun as he did. No explanation has been given for why the officer felt it necessary to draw his gun. Officer Lane then pulled Floyd out of the car and handcuffed him. According to the officer, Floyd resisted.

Lane explained to Floyd—who by all accounts was compliant by this time—that he was being arrested for "passing counterfeit currency." Police body cameras show Floyd being cooperative and repeatedly apologizing to the officers.

It was when officers tried to put Mr. Floyd in their squad car that a struggle ensued. It was 8:19. Floyd began shouting that he was claustrophobic. Obviously, the possibility of having his huge body jammed into the back seat of a squad car, all while wearing handcuffs, terrified the man and caused him to resist. Officers report that Floyd stiffened, fell to the ground, and began crying loudly that he was claustrophobic, begging the officers not to put him in that car.

It was at this time that Officer Derek Chauvin, a supervisor, arrived on the scene. It was also at this time that witnesses began to video the arrest.

Officer Chauvin dragged Floyd to the passenger side of the squad car and, along with other officers, continued to restrain him. This is when Chauvin placed his knee on Floyd's neck. He would keep it there for seven minutes and forty-six seconds. Early reports claimed the duration was eight minutes and forty-six seconds, but those reports were wrong.

It doesn't matter. The seven minutes and forty-six seconds was time enough. It was long enough for Floyd to say he could not breathe more than twenty times. It was time enough for him to plead for his mother and to repeatedly say "please, please, please." It was long enough for the man to fearfully gasp, "You're going to kill me."

In response to this last plea, officer Chauvin replied, "Then stop talking, stop yelling. It takes a heck of a lot of oxygen to talk."

Moments later, Floyd gasped, "I can't believe this, man. Mom, love you. Love you. Tell my kids I love them. I'm dead."

This was when a female bystander shouted to police, "His nose is bleeding! Come on now!"

Six minutes into the seven minutes and forty-six seconds, Floyd became "nonresponsive." He didn't move. He didn't make a sound. Bystanders started screaming for police to check his pulse. Officer Kueng, one of the arresting officers, checked Floyd's wrist but felt nothing. The other officers never moved, never stepped in.

Finally, at 8:27, Officer Chauvin removed his knee from Floyd's neck. An ambulance arrived. A motionless Floyd was rolled onto a gurney and taken to Hennepin County Medical Center. George Floyd was pronounced dead an hour later.

As we all know now, bystander video of the killing of George Floyd went viral. And the world erupted in horror. It is easy to understand why. Most people have never been exposed to a moment in which a man begs for his life but is killed anyway. It might happen in some violent Hollywood epic. Yet seldom have any of us seen a living man, in agony, in tears, begging police for his life. Rarely ever have we seen a man bid his mother goodbye, predict that police were going to kill him, and then, sickeningly, breathe no more.

Here is why I recount this horrifying story—other than to honor the memory of George Floyd. It is to point out how history shapes our responses. You see, most white people haven't had bad experiences with the police. This is just statistically true. They may feel a slight twinge of fear if they are speeding and see a highway patrol car, or if they're driving after they've had too much to drink and a squad car appears in their rearview mirror. Yet white people usually see the police as a force for good and as no threat to the law-abiding.

So when most white people heard of the George Floyd killing, they instinctively asked, "What did the man do wrong? What did he do to bring the police down on him?" Yet when the video of the killing was seen, millions of whites got an education. They saw what an arrest can look like in the black community—though, admittedly, this one was extreme. They heard the pleading. They saw the callous officer mercilessly choking the life out of a man. They heard a man say goodbye to his children and prepare to die.

It changed everything. This is why there has been such a huge response and this is why there were more white people hitting the streets in protest than there were black folks. White people saw what they had never seen before. They understood what it can be like. They felt the injustice, the fear, the utter terror. And they responded.

I'm grateful for all people of every race, skin color, and ethnicity who peacefully worked for change after the George Floyd killing. Still, it is vitally important that all non-blacks understand that blacks view this murder differently. For us, this isn't a one-off. It isn't an outlier. We believe that it is the way of things. It is fruit of a culture that has existed for centuries and still pervades our society today. So the great tragedy is that while most black Americans grieved the death of George Floyd, few black Americans were surprised. For us, any police encounter can end badly, as newspaper headlines have confirmed repeatedly in recent decades.

Again, there is history to this, a history most whites and some blacks may not know. Most formal police departments in the United States began as tools of slave owners to retrieve their runaway slaves. In her *Time* magazine article, "How the U.S. Got Its Police Force," Olivia Waxman observes that though policing in the northern areas of the country began as an effort to protect commercial property, in the South "the economics that drove the creation of police forces were centered not on the protection of shipping interests but on the preservation of the slavery system."[10] Slaves were, after all, not only property but essen-

10 Olivia B. Waxman, "The History of Police in America and the First Force." *Time*, March 6, 2019, time.com/4779112/police-history-origins/.

tial to local economies. So most southern states adopted a pattern of policing drawn from England where sheriffs and constables served the ruling class, the property owners. The North in the U.S. developed differently. The black experience, though, was largely in the South, and so we learned to suspect police. We saw them as being on someone's payroll, under someone's influence, and thus serving something other than true justice.

Now, we aren't stupid. We understand that police departments have evolved. Most police are devoted to public service and committed to doing good in the world. Yet the history is never far from black memory. It doesn't help that you can go on the internet right now and find photos of entire police departments with each officer slyly making a "White Power" sign with their fingers. No, I'm not making this up. Do a search. Trust me, millions of blacks have searched and the photos they find confirm what they have long suspected.

This is the imprint of our history upon us. It is the way a nation built on slavery and slowly emerging from its wake feels to us. It is also why we respond differently from white people to incidents like the George Floyd killing and perhaps even differently from people of other ethnicities.

Let me take this further. It is well-known that black Americans are some of the most patriotic people in the country. Even so, we hear American rhetoric in different ways than non-blacks. We're told the United States is the "land of the free and the home of the brave." We get the brave part. We're not so sure about the free. In fact, most of us think it's a lie. We might hear a politician say that America is the "greatest country on earth." Well, we want to believe it, but we might have a cousin who is living a relatively racism-free life in France or Germany or Jordan. It makes us reconsider. And when we hear someone say,

"God bless America," we tend to think, "Well, he did bless America, but America didn't bless us!"

So we see reality through a different lens than our white friends, and this difference is what our history has left us, has done in us, has made us to be.

As I close this chapter, my reporting of the facts and my emotional response to them as a purely complaint. In fact, my purpose with this entire chapter has not been to merely catalog wrongdoing but rather to tell our story so that our non-black friends can understand. Given a level playing field, African Americans achieve with comparable competency. We are learned and wise, productive and inspiring. We lead well and we innovate. We've proven this again and again. All we expect from our nation is the removal of the yoke of generational oppression and that she would grant us to opportunity to live out the founding creed of this country, "that all men are created equal... and are endowed by their Creator with certain unalienable rights."

I am not claiming some exaggerated victim status when I say that even the cursory survey of African American history I've provided in this chapter shows that blacks are still hoping for what other Americans have by virtue of being Americans. I'm trying to show the systemic bigotry against us during the whole course of American history. I'm also hoping that my non-black friends understand that the meaning of this history has seeped into us. It has set most of our starting place behind the starting line. It has injured our corporate and individual soul. It has sought to damage our spirits.

Yes, we need to fix this together, but what people of my skin color need for non-blacks to understand is our story is different from yours. Our American experience has not been yours. We don't tend to think about words like "police" or "justice" or "equality" or even "America" like our fellow citizens of lighter hue do. This is simply, as the title of this chapter says, "the press of our history upon us."

Now, I know the answer to this. I've seen it work in individual lives and have devoted my life to seeing it work the world over. It is the power that can change hearts. It is the force that can lift the burden of our history from our souls. It is the transformation that can heal what is broken, unify what has been torn apart, and reconnect us to God and each other. I'm talking about the gospel of Jesus Christ—the true, raw, refashioning power of Jesus Christ. This is the answer, I believe. This is the truth that, shed of all the myths men have attached to it, has the power to make us what we were meant to be.

Before I explore with you the power of the gospel of Jesus to change our world, I want to tell you about a project to which I am committed, one that I think can help heal our land.

For many years I have worked to see a National Slave Memorial established in Washington, DC. It has been a long, arduous journey but I am starting to see the idea gain influence with some of our nation's top leaders.

A Slave Memorial would not only honor the suffering of millions of unrecognized Americans who were instrumental in building this country, but it would teach the current generation some vital truths of history. It would solemnify a history of suffering. It would, perhaps, draw some of the poisons out of the lingering memory of slavery, and be a catalyst for substantive conversations that could lead to national health.

The last eighty years have seen memorials to enslaved Africans erected around the country: the Memorial to Enslaved Laborers in Charlottesville, Virginia; the Harriet Tubman Memorial in Manhattan in New York City; and the monument to Frederick Douglass at the University of Maryland, College Park. These are just a few of the valuable assets in the American historical repository honoring those who struggled for freedom.

Still, as tourists stroll the nation's capital, from the Washington Monument to the Lincoln Memorial, there is nothing dedicated to the memory of those who were dehumanized and unthanked. There is nothing on America's National Mall that invites its citizens to ponder the horrors of the economic engine that fueled our nation's growth, while giving them an opportunity to identify with the people who suffered for their gain. It is almost as if some believe that highlighting our nation's most egregious and lengthy injustice would mar our heroic landscape.

On our National Mall, America has a memorial dedicated to the memory of those persecuted European Jews who suffered at the hands of the Nazi regime during World War II: the United States Holocaust Memorial Museum. To journey through this museum is one of the more moving experiences a person can have. Indeed, it is a powerful testament to the effectiveness of history accurately recounted and lives nobly honored. It is a landmark that shouts, "never again!"

As proper as it is for America to remember the horrors of the Holocaust through the establishment of a national museum, our deep commitment to the well-being of the Jewish population worldwide only serves to spotlight our neglect of the inhumanity America inflicted on its black population.

I am fully aware of, and am overwhelmingly grateful for, the National Museum of African American History and Culture prominently placed on the National Mall in Washington, DC. Its establishment and importance should never be minimized. Still, it was not erected for the purpose of healing America's greatest and most longstanding offense. According to the Smithsonian's description, it was established to:

1. Provide an opportunity for those who are interested in African American culture to explore and revel in this history through interactive exhibitions

2. Help all Americans see how their stories, their histories, and their cultures are shaped and informed by global influences

3. Explore what it means to be an American and share how American values like resiliency, optimism, and spirituality are reflected in African American history and culture

4. Serve as a place of collaboration that reaches beyond Washington, DC, to engage new audiences and to work with the myriad of museums and educational institutions that have explored and preserved this important history well before this museum was created[11]

Even with this essential addition to America's historical commemorations, there is a monument conspicuously missing in Washington, DC: The National Enslaved Americans Memorial. The purpose of its establishment would be:

- To acknowledge to the endurance of a people who held on to hope, though there was no reason to do so.

- To thank the slave mother for bearing sons whose bodies she knew were going to be beaten and whose spirits were going to be broken.

---

11 https://nmaahc.si.edu/about/museum

- To be a solemn acknowledgement of the slave who fathered daughters he knew were going to be raped, who would then beget children who looked like the rapist.

- To formally thank those who were the economic backbone of this country for over two hundred years knowing they would never share in the fruit of their labors.

- To memorialize the millions of men and women, created in the image of God, for enduring unspeakable living conditions, intentional under-nourishment, and the selling of their children.

I know that proposing this monument in Washington, DC, is a highly controversial endeavor. Yet, with consciences having been sufficiently pricked by this dream, I am trusting that even the most ambivalent would support and promote filling the memorial gap that remains on our National Mall landscape. I believe the moment for this monument has come.

I think it will change our nation and help turn us toward becoming the people we are called to be.

CHAPTER 4

MORE LIKE HEAVEN
THAN LIKE ME

———————————

Thus far in these pages, I've told you a bit of my story and I've also taken you on a journey through African American history. My goal has been to help those unfamiliar with the backstory of black lives to gain some insight and compassion. I've also hoped to add some understanding for those who are black like me. Yet perhaps the most important thing I've said is that my dreaming in black and white has been inspired by a vision for racial equity and harmony that comes from the Bible; from the clear will of God for the people of the earth to be as one in the purposes of heaven. So allow me to take you to the pages of scripture now, and show you how certain, how vital, and how transforming the biblical view of race has been for me—and can be for us all.

One of the features of the Bible I love the most is the way the merest comment, the slightest reference to something seemingly unimportant can actually be pregnant with meaning. This is the way all great literature is and the Bible is certainly great literature. Yet there is something more. The Bible was written by the Holy Spirit through human beings, and so every word, every side comment, every casual reference has divine meaning—sometimes of a kind that can change the course of history. Let me tell you about one such seemingly insignificant reference, and what it means to me as a black man.

We come to it in the gospels of Matthew, Mark, and Luke. It is only a single sentence in each gospel but it is a sentence filled with divine promise for those who take a moment to go beyond the surface of the words. In fact, the words are so few that I can include each gospel's mention of them here:

> As they were going out, they met a man from Cyrene, named Simon, and they forced him to carry the cross. – Matthew 27:32

> A certain man from Cyrene, Simon, the father of Alexander and Rufus, was passing by on his way in from the country, and they forced him to carry the cross. – Mark 15:21

> As the soldiers led him away, they seized Simon from Cyrene, who was on his way in from the country, and put the cross on him and made him carry it behind Jesus. – Luke 23:26

The moment described in these verses comes as Jesus is carrying his cross through the streets of Jerusalem and to the place of execution. We should remember that by this time, Jesus has already suffered unbelievable violence. He was arrested the previous evening and kept in a dungeon overnight. After he was tried by Jewish leaders and the lead Roman official, Pontius Pilate, he was beaten. This word "beaten" doesn't fully capture the horror that Jesus endured. He had a mocking crown made of long thorns pressed into his skull. He had been punched again and again and then struck repeatedly with rods. Then, he was whipped. I won't go into the details here but let me assure you this was not anything like what you see in Hollywood movies. The whip used— the Romans called it a *flagellum*—had rocks and pieces of iron woven into it and was designed to tear away the flesh.

Then, torn, bruised, and gushing blood, Jesus is made to carry a crossbeam to the place where he will die. He is too weak from what he has endured, though. He stumbles. He drops the beam. Roman soldiers scream at him and hit him in their rage but he cannot do as they demand.

It is just then that another man enters the city. His name is Simon. He has two sons, Rufus and Alexander, we are told. He is just walking into Jerusalem as Jesus, the soldiers, and those following them are walking the other way. The frustrated soldiers do what the Roman law allows them to do. They seize Simon and force him to carry the wooden beam those last steps out of the city and to the place of execution.

That's the story. As I say, it takes only a sentence to invoke all this. But there is one more fact that is mentioned. Simon is from Cyrene. If we are lazy and do not look this up to see what God might be signaling, we are left to believe that Simon is just like any other man in Jerusalem, just an unsuspecting passerby forced to do an unpleasant task under the angry eyes of Roman soldiers.

The key word, though, is Cyrene. It was the chief city in Libya at that time, a land in North Africa. It sat halfway between the two larger cities of Alexandria and Carthage.

Did you catch it, though? Cyrene was a city in Africa. Simon, a man from that city, helped Jesus carry the cross. He would have looked into those eyes. The blood of the Son of God might have fallen upon him. He would have borne across his shoulders the instrument by which God's son liberated the world.

A man from Africa. It's unbelievably important. We can't know for sure what his exact skin color was. He might have been black, but he was definitely from Africa.

If you are not black, imagine something for a moment. Imagine that you are black, perhaps a young black man like I was when I encountered this story, and society has told you all your life that everything African is defective. Everything African is lesser and flawed, ugly and disgusting. You are meant to be ashamed. You are supposed to think yourself inferior.

Then you read your Bible. You come upon a passage in which a man from Africa—that supposedly "dark" and "shameful" place—is made part of the Easter story.

It changes you. You feel pride and joy, a sense that God somehow signaled his noble purposes for Africa and black human beings by making a black man part of the Jesus story. In fact, I don't mind telling you that Simon of Cyrene is one of my heroes. Learning of his story and a bit of his background helped to set me free as a black man. All I had ever seen is what you've seen: the movies and Christian art in which Jesus is white, the disciples are even whiter and for some reason have British accents, and darn near every depiction of anyone important in Church history is played by an actor with blond hair and blue eyes.

Then comes my man Simon of Cyrene. He's African. He's from that soil. He's of that people. He may be a transplant. I don't care. He's African. He might even be black. He's definitely darker than the dudes in the movies or the paintings on the walls of most churches or the great art of the Western world in which hardly any blacks or Africans ever appear. If blacks do appear, they're naked, stupid looking, and carrying some white guy's luggage.

Simon of Cyrene changed me. Why? Because Roman soldiers didn't involve him in the crucifixion story on their own. God made that happen. He was telling me and all who look like me something important. It has echoed through history. It has lit up the souls of black folks all over the world.

That's not all there is to the story. You see, Simon of Cyrene just might appear again in the New Testament. If so, we get even more information about him.

The mention comes in Acts, chapter 13. We are being told who the "prophets and teachers" are in the church of Antioch. I should jump ahead of the story a bit and say that Antioch is on the verge of being the lead missionary-sending church of the entire early Christian era, so who is leading them at this point is really important.

One of the men in the list is "Simeon called Niger." Simeon is simply the Hebrew version of the name Simon, so some scholars believe this is the same Simon of Cyrene who helped Jesus carry the cross. If it is, two very important facts emerge.

The first is that Simon is a black man. You see in this verse that it says, "Simeon called Niger." Some folks read this as though it says, "Simeon from Niger." Yet that wouldn't make any sense. The country of Niger didn't exist until 1960 and the river that gives the nation its name wasn't called Niger until the 1500s.

No, the word Niger (NY-jer) means "black." The Simeon who was a leader at Antioch in the early church wasn't from Niger, he was black. This means that if he is the same Simeon or Simon who helped Jesus, as some scholars suspect, then a black man from Africa carried the cross on which the Son of God set the world free.

Second, it also means that a black man was a prophet or teacher at the most important missionary-sending church of the time. It means that the Christian movement started out integrated and multiracial/multiethnic in a way that is rare today.

In fact, let's look at the whole list of the leaders at Antioch in Acts 13:1. The first is Barnabas, who we know is a Jewish man (a Levite) from the Island of Cyprus.[12] The next man is "Simeon called Niger." Then comes Lucius of Cyrene. Well, we already know where Cyrene is. It's in Africa. Whatever the skin color of Lucius was, he was from the continent of Africa. Then there is Manaen, whom we are told grew up with Herod the tetrarch. He was probably a Greek Jew who was raised with Herod or was his foster brother. Then, there is Paul, who we know was a Jew from Tarsus, a city on what is now the southern coast of Turkey.

Think of it. These are the prophets and teachers in a single church. There is a black man, an African man of unknown color, a Greek aristocrat, a Jew from Cyprus, and another Jew from Tarsus among them. None of these folks are from Antioch. They are multinational. They are multiethnic. They are multilingual. They are of various skin colors.

This was the way the early church looked. This was the vision that set the nations aflame. Jesus had said go into all the world and make disciples. The early Christians did. Yet no one asked what color these disciples were going to be. Few thought in terms of one race being holier than another because of skin color. The church of Antioch reveals this and it is all recorded in the pages of scripture itself. I could describe

---

12 Acts 4:36

what we know of other churches in early Christian history and you would see the same.

It's also important to know that the region of Africa which Simon was from, the region of North Africa, was so influential in the first centuries of Christianity that some modern scholars say that North African Christianity set the trajectory for the faith. And, yes, there were men and women of black skin among them.

Do you feel convicted by this? I do. If there was a church today with a black man, a Greek man, a man from Cyprus, a man from Turkey, and a man from Africa in the leadership, people would find it remarkable. Folks would travel to that church to see how they pulled it off. And yet such a leadership shouldn't be an oddity. It should be the norm. It should be routine. It was, after all, the way things were at the beginning. We messed it up through the centuries, because we allowed the kingdom of darkness to plant a vile spirit of separatism in our hearts.

Now if these two appearances of Simon in the Bible—one when Jesus was heading to the cross, the other among a multiracial team of leaders—were all there was in the entire Bible, it would have been enough for me and for millions who look like me to get the signal God was sending. Yet these verses are just a few of the ones that speak of blacks and Africans as part of God's plan, as central to his strategy for reclaiming the earth for his purposes.

One of my favorite progressions in scripture, and one that powerfully reveals God's reaching to Africa and blacks, is in the constant references to Ethiopia. It is as though God is excited about Ethiopia and Africa as a whole coming to him. He's like an eager father talking about the soon arrival of his African people just about every time he has a chance. Just listen to a few of these moments. To understand them, you have to know that Ethiopia was in the region that is called Cush in the Bible.

Cush will submit herself to God – Psalm 68:31

In that day the Lord will reach out his hand a second time to reclaim the surviving remnant of his people from Assyria, from Lower Egypt, from Upper Egypt, from Cush... – Isaiah 11:11

From beyond the rivers of Cush, my worshipers, my scattered people, will bring me offerings. – Zephaniah 3:10

And so it goes. In addition to these references, there is the grand story of the Queen of Sheba visiting King Solomon during his reign over Israel. Now, Sheba was likely a kingdom in southwest Arabia. This meant it was near Ethiopia, and eastern Africa would have influenced her not only through trade but also through cultural exchange. We are told in I Kings 10 that the queen decided to visit Solomon because she had heard of his fame and his "relationship to the Lord." She wanted to test Solomon with "hard questions," so she arrived with a huge caravan of gifts, eager to explore both the kingdom and the wise man she had heard so much about.

We are told that Solomon answered all her questions and that nothing the queen asked about was too hard for him to explain. Solomon also made sure his visitor saw the palace he had built, tasted his magnificent food, met his grand officials, and even witnessed the worship of the Lord in the Temple.

The queen was overwhelmed by what she saw. The words she gave in delighted tribute are worth quoting in full:

*The report I heard in my own country about your achievements
and your wisdom is true. But I did not believe these things until I
came and saw with my own eyes. Indeed, not even half was told
me; in wisdom and wealth you have far exceeded the report I
heard. How happy your people must be? How happy your officials,
who continually stand before you and hear your wisdom. Praise be
to the Lord your God, who has delighted in you and placed you on
the throne of Israel. Because of the Lord's eternal love for Israel, he
has made you king to maintain justice and righteousness.*[13]

We can tell by these words that the Queen of Sheba saw what
Solomon's relationship with God and God's love for Israel produced.
She saw justice. She saw righteousness. She saw stunning prosperity
and surely felt the presence of the one true God. Then, after an opu-
lent exchange of gifts by the two sovereigns, the queen returned to her
country.

We are not told specifically what happened then, but we can venture an educated guess. The queen would not have returned to her land
and kept her mouth shut. Nor would the hundreds who had made the
trip with her. She would have described it all and she would have begun
to bring her land into harmony with what she saw. Solomon's wisdom,
his leadership, his principles, his judgement, and his grasp of divine justice would have been transplanted to the Queen of Sheba. It is not going
too far to imagine that the worship of Jehovah would have taken root
under the queen's hand. And all of it, the wisdom, the practices, and the
worship, would have begun to spread throughout the region.

Knowing all this background allows us to jump ahead to a moving story in the book of Acts. Keep in mind, now, we are talking about

---

13 I Kings 10:6-9, NIV

God reaching to Africa. We are told in Acts 8:26 that Philip, one of the deacons who the apostles appointed in the church of Jerusalem, has been instructed by God to head to Gaza by a desert road. As he does, he sees a an official of the Queen of Ethiopia sitting in a chariot and reading the book of Isaiah.

We should picture the scene. The man is a high official. He is in grand clothes. His chariot is the size of a modern minivan and is adorned beautifully. He is surely surrounded by troops as he sits by the side of the road reading.

Philip is told by the Holy Spirit to go stand near the chariot. This is risky but he does it. He hears the man reading out loud. He's reading Isaiah 53, the poetic chapter about Jesus as the suffering servant. Philip asks him if he knows what he's reading. The man seems frustrated. He says, "How can I unless someone explains it to me?" Then the man pleads for Philip to teach him.

Now there is a backstory here. We've been told that this Ethiopian eunuch has just come from Jerusalem where he worshipped God. What we now know through the blessings of archaeology is that when this man went to worship God at the Temple, he would have been kept in the most outer portions of the Temple grounds and he would likely have seen a sign of the kind that has been recovered today by archaeologists: a stone that was embedded in the Temple fence. Listen to the harsh words:

> *Foreigners must not enter inside the balustrade or into the forecourt around the sanctuary. Whoever is caught will have himself to blame for his ensuing death.*

Imagine the Ethiopian eunuch's frustration. He is a Gentile God-seeker. This is likely part of the faith that has permeated his homeland, probably a faith that was first planted in his region by the Queen of Sheba centuries before. He travels to Jerusalem to worship the Lord. It is a big moment for him, but he is kept at a distance, made to worship nearly in the streets, and he sees a sign that threatens him with his life if he, a foreigner, dares to enter the forecourt around the sanctuary. Quite a welcome!

Still, he travels home reading about the Messiah and asking questions. That's when God positions Philip at just the right time to teach the man about Jesus. The Bible tells us that the man receives the "good news" and is baptized.

Take a moment and consider what this story might mean to people who look like me. God has said repeatedly throughout the Old Testament that he is eager for those in Cush and beyond to come to him. He has sent the Queen of Sheba to learn from Solomon about all that comes from his relationship with the Lord. Then, centuries later, when an Ethiopian official goes to Jerusalem to worship, God positions Philip the Evangelist at just the right time and at just the right place on a desert road so he can intercept the man, explain the gospel to him, and baptize him before sending the man on his way back to Ethiopia.

What's the lesson? God is reaching to Africa. God wants to draw people who look like me to himself. God is working elaborate plans throughout history to make sure his truth, his love, and his ways of running nations are planted in Ethiopia and the lands of Africa well beyond.

Now, I understand this is a historical truth many of us already know. But, again, just imagine a person who is black and who has been told that God made him only for slavery and servitude, that it is the divine order that he is always second-class, always in the back of the bus—literally! Then he reads about God's centuries-long efforts to reach the African people. He sees himself in the pages of scripture. He understands what it means that men like Simon of Cyrene and the Ethiopian eunuch have such prominent places in God's book. He gets what God is saying. *I love you. I want you with me. You are not less or inferior or defective or cursed. You are on my mind, in my heart, and at the forefront of my purposes for the world.*

If you are that black person reading this, if you are young Brett Fuller coming upon this for the first time, it changes you. A lie is exposed. A falsehood people have been trying to press into your soul and the souls of blacks for centuries is exploded. You see things as they are, and you shout your praise to God that he has set you free.

By the way, I'll leave you to read about the history of Christianity in Ethiopia on your own, but let me just tell you one fact that will hint at what God did in that land. During World War II, the famous and beloved emperor of Ethiopia, Haile Selassie, was a heroic figure because he stood against the fascist Italian occupation of his nation. It's an amazing story. Guess what one of his ceremonial names was? Lion of the Tribe of Judah. Although the reverence given by his followers often wrongly rivals the true Lion of the Tribe of Judah, Jesus, the fact that the verbiage by which they reference their hero harkens from Scripture, speaks volumes. From facts like this and the amazing history of Christianity in Ethiopia, we can surmise that the Ethiopian eunuch on that desert road went back to his homeland, shared the faith that Philip taught him, and changed his nation. A vital Christian faith lives there to this day, with believers thinking of themselves as conquerors in the name of the Lion of Judah—Jesus.

Stories like this mean everything to people like me, people of my skin color and background, and mainly because we had a lie pressed on us early in our history, a lie that was a distortion of a biblical event. It may be hard for some non-blacks to understand this but let me try to explain.

There is an odd story in Genesis 9 in which Noah, the hero of the famous Ark, drank too much wine and lay in his bed naked. Noah had three sons: Ham, Shem, and Japheth. Ham wandered into Noah's bedroom and happened to see his father naked. He then went and told his two brothers, Shem and Japheth, what he had seen. These two brothers put a cloth over themselves, walked backward into their father's room, and covered Noah without ever seeing him naked.

When Noah woke up from his drunken slumber, he was furious with Ham. Strangely, here is what he said:

Cursed be Canaan! The lowest of slaves will he be to his brothers.

Then, while speaking blessings on Shem and Japheth, Noah says, "May Canaan be the slave of Shem," and "May Canaan be the slave of Japheth."

I should explain that Canaan is one of Ham's sons. He had others. They were Cush, Put, and Egypt. These men, of course, had sons also and so it went for generations. Yet the only son that Noah cursed was Canaan. Ham wasn't cursed. Put wasn't cursed. Egypt wasn't cursed. Only Canaan. I can't tell you why. Nor can even the best Bible scholars.

What I can tell you is that the curse Noah spoke over Canaan has been laid on Ham throughout history. Why is this important? Because Ham is the ancestor of the folks who went south and populated Africa. So if you aren't careful about what the Bible says, you can distort scripture and try to make the case that Ham is cursed by God and therefore all people with black skin are cursed. If you believe all this, then you might also believe that all blacks are to be slaves to the rest of humanity. That's what the idiot version of Noah's curse might leave you with.

This would all be just an insignificant oddity from the pages of scripture except that this lie—that all blacks are cursed by God and are doomed to be the slaves for the rest of mankind—has fueled black holocausts. It was while they spouted Noah's curse as their justification that the Christians of Europe began making slaves of Africans. You can even read much about the "Curse of the Hamites" in the newspapers and theology books of the American South before the Civil War. In fact, entire denominations had this view as a cardinal doctrine until relatively recently. This was also the belief of Joseph Smith, the founder of the Church of Jesus Christ of Latter Day Saints, the Mormons, and it wasn't discarded by that religious group until 1978.

In short, it is a lie that has done untold damage to an entire race and it is all drawn from a distortion of scripture, found in a passage that is difficult to understand, that has been manipulated to destroy generations of people with black skin.

So try to feel with me what it must have been like for an African American man of an earlier generation to hear that the Bible that had been used to enslave him actually speaks of him as called, chosen, loved, and commissioned to do great things. It was the Good News in every sense and it was truth that changed the world—and is still changing it!

We've seen then that a few words in scripture have set black people free and that a few distorted words have led to their bondage. Let me turn the diamond of this topic and show you a sweet and tender type of liberation for African Americans that came from just three words in the Bible.

In the Song of Solomon, that poetic look at human love that may also typify the love of God for all mankind, there is a single verse that has come to have vast meaning for some blacks, African Americans in particular. In the first chapter and the fifth verse of that book, a woman says something that lands in English as close to these words: "I am dark, but lovely." Now, there are many versions of these words. The old King James Version makes them, "I am black but comely." The New King James says, "I am dark, but lovely." More modern translations, like the New Living Translation, renders them as "I am dark but beautiful."

Frankly, it doesn't matter what the exact words are. Black people don't care! What they know is that someone in the Bible has said that black or dark or whatever is beautiful or comely or lovely—just something good!

I'll tell you something else before I explain what all this has meant to us. The Song of Solomon also tells us that this woman who is dark was likely not dark from birth but from being in the sun. The very next verse after the one that has the woman saying, "Dark am I, yet lovely" (this is the New International Version's approach) has the woman also saying, "Do not stare at me because I am dark, because I am darkened by the sun."[14]

I'll tell you frankly, black people don't care why this woman was dark. They aren't doing a scholar's exegesis of the verse. They are hearing something most non-blacks don't because most non-blacks have not been told their skin color is ugly. Blacks have been told this throughout most of human history. So they don't care if this woman in the Song of Solomon is dark because she stood too close to the microwave or spent too much time at the beach. The simple fact is that in a book inspired by the Holy Spirit, someone said that dark is lovely. This, believe me, is

---

14 Song of Solomon 1:6, NIV

liberating. It is enough to move you to tears. It means that dark is not disgusting, that human beings aren't all living on a scale from white to black, from good to bad, from beautiful to repulsive. Black is beautiful too.

You might think I'm overstating the importance of this. I'm not. What we have to understand is that throughout much of history, dark skin meant lower class, workers in the field, and even cursed, as we've seen. Even today in Asian countries like Japan and Vietnam, women will wear sun visors, face masks, hats, and gloves to the elbow all in an attempt to avoid the sun. Why? It's because they live in a culture which sees light skin as beautiful and darker skin as belonging to the lower classes—those who work in the fields under the blazing sun and are thus less attractive. These Asians aren't being racists. They are simply trying to look like what their culture tells them is beautiful. Yet where does this leave folks who look like me? What if a culture that prizes light skin and denigrates dark skin covers the whole planet? Then I am ugly, or at least less desirable. So is my wife. So are my children. So is everyone with dark skin.

Most of us know that this was the attitude toward darker skin that pervaded the United States until the 1960s and 1970s when some folks finally started saying, "Black is Beautiful." Part of what inspired this were the words we've already seen in Song of Solomon 1:5. My mother, for example, didn't know much scripture by heart but, trust me, she knew "dark but lovely." I heard those words in my house over and over again. They were beloved. I've also heard them from my wife and my daughters.

Yet you don't have to take my word for it. Go online and search for the words "Dark & Lovely." You are going to discover a virtual empire of hair products for black women, all named in the same spirit in which

Solomon penned his beloved's words—whether the folks buying these products know scripture or not.

I've been warned by the women in my family not to talk like I'm an expert on black women's hair. That is definitely a world that a man, even a black man, doesn't want to venture into lightly. So, I'll keep my distance. Still, I have to say this. Beyond the exact products black women use and what the names of those products are, there is the wonderfully liberating truth that black hair is magnificent.

It is important to know that the natural hair of black people was something to be ashamed of not that long ago. White culture, white styles, white "looks"—patterned by Vogue magazine and Barbie Dolls—made black women feel that straight, white women's hair, was all that was beautiful. That has changed now, thank God. The "Black is Beautiful" movement, the development of hair products for black women, and the rise of beautiful black models in the fashion world have all led to a new day.

So those simple three words—Dark and Lovely—meant everything to blacks who came from a heritage of self-loathing for how they looked. It's a new day, a day inspired by three words buried deep in the Old Testament. That's how little it took to undo the damage done and cause us to know the wonder of how God made us.

I'll take this one step further. We not only can celebrate black or dark skin today, we can celebrate the flared nose, the thick lips, the natural hair of our people. This is the design of God, in the same way that common Anglo features, Asian features, Hispanic features, and all ethnic features were created by God. It is all his artwork, all created to glorify him. How dare any man say it is ugly or cursed or disgusting? I glorify God by being—and looking—as I am made to look by a loving

Father. I encourage everyone in my sphere of influence to do the same with their looks.

My white friends, I understand you've likely never had most of these ideas in your head even once in your life. I know. I get it. Yet part of you understanding us is that you learn to think these thoughts, recognize this meaning, and let this heritage impact you. That's how we know each other. That's how we lose our hearts to each other. That's how we cease being adversaries and become advocates for each other.

I've been talking about specific verses and people in the Bible. Let's go beyond that. Let's talk about the overall story, the narrative arc of the Bible. This is the big picture we are meant to grasp and so it really outweighs any specific person or a few words we find in the pages of scripture.

What God wanted all along was for mankind in all its diversity to live in relationship with him and to live together in the paradise of the earth. As we can easily see in the first chapters of the Bible, man messed this up. He rebelled against God. He killed his fellow man. He started living in all types of perversion and sin. So, God began a great reclamation project. He wanted to get mankind back into relationship with him and back into being the regents on earth he had designed them to be.

As we read of this reclamation project in scripture, God begins with Israel. These words are important. God *begins* with Israel. He calls their ancestors out of pagan lands, places them in the promised land, teaches them his law and his ways, and through the centuries sends them prophets, deliverers, and champions. He even uses foreign kings and nations on their behalf. He loves them. He woos them. He restores them when they stray. He blesses and protects them time and again. This is largely the story we read throughout the Old Testament.

Then comes Jesus Christ. He is the Messiah predicted often in the Old Testament, the one who will restore all things. He comes, he teaches, he performs miracles, and he dies for all mankind. A church is born. It is told to go into all the world and make disciples of all nations.

Here comes the problem. Israel has been God's tool for centuries. They are the first, but now they have to learn they aren't the only. After Jesus and with the birth of the Christian church, God is reaching to the whole world, Israel included but not Israel alone.

This creates a crisis for the early Church. We read of it first in Acts 15. Paul and Barnabas had begun leading non-Jews to Jesus. A question arose: Can these Gentile believers come directly to faith in Jesus, or do they have to be Jews first? Do they have to observe the law and be circumcised and do all the things God had been requiring of the Jews for centuries? In short, can the Gentiles become Christians without having to become Jews first?

The answer of the Council of Jerusalem in Acts 15, of the leaders of the church at the time, was, "Yes, Gentiles can become Christians without becoming Jews first. They should be moral, but they do not have to be Jews before believing in Jesus."

It was a huge moment for the cause of the Gospel. It required people to believe that God had used Israel first but he did not intend to reach Israel only. He cared about the nations outside of Israel. He longed for them to be restored to him along with Israel. That's why the Great Commission of Matthew 28:18–20 commands going into "all nations." That's why on the Day of Pentecost, the day the Holy Spirit came upon the early Church, there were more than a dozen different people groups standing by, witnessing, and eventually participating. Let's read the list straight from the Bible to get the impact:

Parthians, Medes and Elamites; residents of Mesopotamia, Judea
and Cappadocia, Pontus and Asia, Phrygia and Pamphylia, Egypt
and the parts of Libya near Cyrene; visitors from Rome, (both
Jews and converts to Judaism); Cretans and Arabs—we hear them
declaring the wonders of God in our own tongues![15]

Now, this inclusion of non-Jews in God's plan caused some problems for Christians who were of Jewish background. God had to deal with them decisively to move them forward in his purposes. We are given a bird's-eye view of this in the life of Peter.

We should remember that Peter was a fisherman and also a devoted Jew. His heritage was Jewish, his culture was Jewish, and it is not going too far to say that his soul was Jewish. He served God and kept the commandments. When the time came for Peter to understand God's broader purposes—that God used Israel first but did not intend to use Israel only—this disciple of Jesus had a hard time.

So God intervened. We witness the moment of change when Peter is on a rooftop terrace one day in the seaside city of Joppa. We are told in Acts 10:11–16 that God opened the heavens to Peter and something like a large sheet was lowered before him with animals that had traditionally been unclean or forbidden for the Jews. A voice said, "Get up, Peter. Kill and eat." Peter replied, "Surely not, Lord! I have never eaten anything impure or unclean." Then the voice said, "Do not call anything impure that God has made clean." This happened three times.

Clearly, God was not really speaking to Peter primarily about food. He was speaking to him about considering everything outside of Israel to be unclean—people, food, land, all of it. We are told that Peter was just pondering what the vision meant when men knocked at the

---

15 Acts 2:10-11,

door of the house where he was staying and asked to see him. When Peter was informed of it, the Holy Spirit spoke to him and said, "Simon, three men are looking for you. So get up and go downstairs. Do not hesitate to go with them, for I have sent them."

History turned on this moment. The men at the door were non-Jews. They were Gentiles. Peter went with them, entered their house—something forbidden under the law—and preached the gospel to them. As he did, the Holy Spirit fell upon all who were gathered. This is often called The Gentile Pentecost. The experience confirmed to the early Church that God was indeed reaching to the non-Jewish world to bring all—Jew and non-Jew—to himself.

Peter's process of change is exposed to us. Paul's is not. Yet we know it happened. Why? Well, listen to the things he says about what we would call today "inclusion"—about the old limits and boundaries being expanded to all the world.

Or is God the God of Jews only? Is he not the God of Gentiles too? Yes, of Gentiles too. - Romans 3:29

For we were all baptized by one Spirit so as to form one body—whether Jews or Gentiles, slave or free—and we were all given the one Spirit to drink. - 1 Corinthians 12:13

There is neither Jew nor Gentile, neither slave nor free, nor is there male and female, for you are all one in Christ Jesus. - Galatians 3:28

Here there is no Gentile or Jew, circumcised or uncircumcised, barbarian, Scythian, slave or free, but Christ is all, and is in all. - Colossians 3:11

You see, then, that while we do not have the hidden camera on Paul's change about inclusion that we had on Peter's change, it clearly happened. Keep in mind that Paul said himself that he was an extremist about being a Jew. Listen to his own words.

> *If someone else thinks they have reasons to put confidence in the flesh, I have more: circumcised on the eighth day, of the people of Israel, of the tribe of Benjamin, a Hebrew of Hebrews; in regard to the law, a Pharisee; as for zeal, persecuting the church; as for righteousness based on the law, faultless.*[16]

So Paul tells us that he was a "super-Jew" in his early life, pursuing all things Jewish with passion and zeal. Then Jesus interrupted his life. The Lord saved Paul and called him to be an apostle to the Gentiles. A massive change had to happen. Paul had to understand that God may have used Israel first but that God had no intention of using Israel only. He wanted to reach through Israel to the nations of the world. So Paul, an extremist Jewish leader, became the Apostle to the Great Unwashed, to the Great Unclean, to those most Jews thought were outcasts.

This is what the gospel is meant to produce: a transformation in our thinking about race, about ethnicity, even about God using males and females, and certainly about who is unclean religiously and who is not.

Remember the vision that ought to influence everything we think and do about such things. Remember the words I have already quoted from John's vision of heavenly realities in the book of Revelation: "After this I looked, and there before me was a great multitude that no one could count, from every nation, tribe, people and language, standing

---

16 Philippians 3:4-6, NIV

before the throne and before the Lamb."[17] This is where God chooses to enthrone himself. This is what God is working to accomplish. And this is not only the vision we are meant to have of things in heaven, but it is the vision we are meant to be working toward here on earth.

Now, I could go on for pages. I could tell you about other people mentioned in the Bible who might be black. Some scholars think that the wife of Moses, a woman named Zipporah, was black. She was, after all, a Cushite, which means she was from the region around modern Sudan and Ethiopia.[18] There are scholars who also believe that Bathsheba, King David's lover and wife, was black. Or, I could leave scripture and talk about what we know about the early Church. Do you know that in the catacombs in Rome, those underground caverns where early Christians worshipped in secret and were buried, there is art on the walls depicting black Christians? This means that once again, "we were there," and not just on the side but integral and woven into the life of the believers of that time. And so it goes through all generations of believers.

I have to stop and ask the question: How did we fall so far? How did we start with a faith meant to embrace all people, and end up with a faith in which people of color are locked out of churches, kept from leadership, and, during some periods in American history, even thought not to have souls or even be human? How did we fall so far?

I can't fully answer that question beyond what I've already said here. Yet whether I can fully explain the sinfulness of human hearts or not, I want to fix it. I want to heal the disease. I want you to do it with me.

Let me finish this chapter with an episode from the life of Jesus which, if understood correctly, helps us see his zeal about this matter

---

17 Revelation 7:9, NIV
18 Numbers 12:1, NIV

of righteous inclusion. It is an episode that happened twice, once at the beginning of his ministry, and once just at the end. Here is the account from the start of his ministry:

> *In the temple courts he found people selling cattle, sheep and doves, and others sitting at table exchanging money. So he made a whip out of cords, and drove all from the temple courts, both sheep and cattle; he scattered the coins of the money changers and overturned their tables. To those who sold doves he said, "Get these out of here! Stop turning my Father's house into a market!"[19]*

Here is the account from the episode at the end of his ministry:

> *On reaching Jerusalem, Jesus entered the temple courts and began driving out those who were buying and selling there. He overturned the tables of the money changers and the benches of those selling doves, and would not allow anyone to carry merchandise through the temple courts. And as he taught them, he said, "Is it not written: 'My house will be called a house of prayer for all nations?' But you have made it a 'den of robbers.'"[20]*

We love seeing our hero Jesus battle evildoers. We love seeing him bold and physical and filled with zeal for his God. Yet do we know what the real issue is here?

Usually Christians have concluded that Jesus was upset that money was being exchanged or that things were being sold near the temple. Not true. This trade was God ordained. A pilgrim coming from far off to sacrifice in Jerusalem could simply bring money rather than

---

19 John 2:14–16, NIV
20 Mark 11:15–17, NIV

walk a sheep or carry a cage of doves from a distant country. Then, when he got to the Temple, he exchanged his local currency for the Temple currency and used his new money to buy whatever animal he wanted to sacrifice. All this was allowed.

So what was Jesus so angry about? Well, in their callousness, the money changers and sellers had moved their otherwise legitimate business into the Court of the Gentiles, the only place that the Gentiles had to pray. This was a form of bigotry. It was a form of racial pride. *We Jews can keep the Great Unwashed Gentiles from God. We can do our trade even if it keeps the Gentiles from having a place in the presence of God.*

Jesus saw this and was furious. The heartlessness! The ignorance of God's purposes! The racism! And so he upends it all.

It is the words he speaks that give us the clue. You see, in some of the gospel accounts, Jesus only says, "Stop turning my father's house into a market." This is what we read in the gospel of John, for example. Yet Mark comes to our rescue. He adds the all-important words: "My father's house will be called a house of prayer *for all nations.*" There it is! "For all nations." Jesus isn't angry about the business being conducted. He's angry about where it is being conducted—in the only place the Gentiles have to pray and in the only temple of the living God on earth. It is the systemic bigotry that makes Jesus as angry as we ever see him. It is the heartless racism that makes him fashion a whip, get fiercely in the face of those carrying goods through the Court of the Gentiles, and send tables flying.

It is important to note that though Christ's zeal for his father's house was aggressive, is was not violent (it is thought that he used the handmade whip not on people, but as a tool to help force the larger animals out of the temple courts). He was assertive, but not destructive. He temporarily interrupted business done in the wrong place without permanently damaging Jewish commerce. People were inconvenienced, but no one was injured. The precision with which he conducted his assault on the lack of space the Jews were affording the prayerful Gentiles was masterful.

I love it, don't you? Especially now that we are clear on what Jesus is so passionate about.

Here's my point. Let's be as fierce in our day against what angered Jesus just as Jesus was in his time. Let's be bold, aggressive, proactive, on fire to see the walls of division and bigotry broken down.

We've seen enough from the Bible just in this short chapter to know for certain that God is reaching to every kind of person on earth. We should be too. So should our churches. And the result should be respect and justice for all of us.

Let's commit ourselves to it. Let's make the changes we need to make. And let's do it in our generation.

Now, let's start talking solutions.

CHAPTER 5

RETOOLING FOR RECONCILIATION

A s important as all we have talked about has been, we've been flying at 35,000 feet. We've been looking at the big picture. Now it's time to land the plane and get busy changing the world on the ground.

I must warn you, though, that I'm going to hit hard in these next two chapters. I'm going to be real and uncomfortably frank. I'm going to push in on your biases, put some salty truth in your wounds, and call you up to a higher level of living. As a participant in collegiate athletics and a chaplain of a professional football team, I've seen lots of coaches use colorful methods to motivate their players. Why? They want them to be their best. They are willing to hurt their feelings to make them better on the field. That's what I'm attempting to do here.

Another caution before we begin. What follows is all about changing cultures of racism and social inequities. It is about reworking institutions and doing so after we have allowed God to rework our hearts. The next two chapters will map the difficult path that is the road to healing. The tolls are pricey, but for me the destination has been more than worth the cost. Of course, you will have to decide for yourself.

The first thing I look for, whether I'm talking to a person who says they want to make a change or I'm consulting with the leaders of an organization, is this: What is the motive for seeking change? Why are you asking me for help?

There is a pastor in my community who called me soon after the racial troubles of 2020 began. He asked, "Are you surprised by what's going on?" I said, "No. I'm not surprised, nor am I surprised that you would ask that question. In fact, do you know that this is the first time you've ever called me?"

I don't make a practice of mincing words when the subjects of the black experience and ethnic injustice come up. I never sacrifice kindness when addressing the issue, but I rarely spare people's feelings, particularly the feelings of influential leaders, when they ask me what I think. My aim is not merely to right wrongs or to right wrong thinking, but to right hearts.

The conversation with that man continued. I said to him, "You're calling me because your world is being upset. You aren't calling me because George Floyd died and you're not calling me because Ahmaud Aubrey was murdered. You're also not calling me because black people are being choked out on the streets."

The gentleman was a little dismayed. I went on. "You didn't pick up the phone because you're concerned about people who look like me. You're concerned for people who look like you. You must understand that as a kingdom representative, this motivation won't serve you or your community well. As a pastor to the broader community, you must develop the ability to feel the pain of your entire community, not just the part of it with which you ethnically identify. You need to care about something bigger than yourself and the folks who look like you. You've got to understand that black folks are tired, in pain, and white folks haven't been listening. But if you're ready to go beyond where you've been before, I'll help you."

I speak like this because I'm operating from a certain basis of understanding. Let me break it out for you.

In working with people on ethnic issues, I've got my radar turned on to detect three things. The first, but not the most important, is prejudice. This is simply belief before the facts. It is assumption in absence of facts. If no other factors are at work, prejudice is dealt with by providing facts. You get the accurate necessary information, now you know, and prejudice should be banished.

The next force my radar is bigotry. Simply put, bigotry is malevolent prejudice. It is hatred and opposition with the intent to harm. This is the KKK. This is the Skinhead movement. This is hardcore hating racists all through the world. Their problem is not fixed by providing accurate information. It is not fixed by pointing out their prejudice. It is only fixed by a heart change. Something—and I believe it has to be God and his truth—has to intervene and rewire the inner systems of belief and response in the human heart.

Finally there is racism. This is bigotry and antagonism codified, in print and/or in culture. It is hatred and opposition worked into a system and woven into a society. It perpetuates itself. It feeds on itself. It grows. It is a system that works itself out in every area of life. It also—and this is important—can shape a person without them really being aware of it.

Many people in American society are like this. They've lived in a certain culture. That culture may be getting better in some places and worse in others, but it is shaping the people in it all day, every day. So, if they're living in a racist culture they can be conditioned in ways they may not even recognize. Someone has to help them see, however dramatically, that they are being made into something they do not understand and may not want.

This may help you understand why I choose to be compassionately straightforward with people when trying to bring change. Look at the three solutions to the problems I just listed. For prejudice, there has to be a giving of facts. For bigotry, there has to be a confrontation with the hate, and a working under God's hand to make a change. For racism, there has to be an exposure of the system and the culture—the temperature of the water—the individual has been living in. None of these responses are best done in a whisper. None of them are accomplished with a pleading, "aw shucks" approach. It takes clarity. It takes merciful firmness. It takes risking offense. It's worth it, though. The prize is worth the price.

It is important for me to point out how insidious and evil racist cultures can be. Let me take as an example something that is taught in nearly every school in the country. I'm talking about Darwinism.

Usually, the great debate about Darwinism has to do with the difference between the idea that God created all things and the Darwinian idea that all life evolved. So, you might expect that since I'm a pastor, I'm going to go off on Mr. Darwin for denying the book of Genesis and daring to suggest that God didn't create man but that he evolved from lower life forms.

I'm happy to have that debate at some other time. Right now, though, in these pages, I'm not talking about creationism versus evolution. I'm talking about Darwin's pure racism and the fact that this racism is taught as truth all throughout our nation. It's in the water. It is the acrid smell to which we have become accustomed. It's part of the culture.

Everyone who has read and understood Charles Darwin knows that he was among the first people to base the idea of racial inequality on a philosophy to which most of the world now adheres: evolution. Although a staunch abolitionist, Darwin's eagerness to see the enslaved African free failed to curb his leaning toward white supremacy. Steven Rose, Professor of Biology and Neurobiology at Open University in the United Kingdom says,

> "Darwin was, after all, a man of his time, class and society.
> True, he was committed to a monogenic, rather than the
> prevailing polygenic, view of human origins, but he still divided
> humanity into distinct races according to differences in skin,
> eye or hair colour. He was also convinced that evolution
> was progressive, and that the white races—especially the
> Europeans—were evolutionarily more advanced than the black
> races, thus establishing race differences and a racial hierarchy."[21]

Darwin's theory of evolution teaches that mankind progressed through various stages of evolution. In this scheme, Darwin taught that blacks are on the downside of evolution, which means less evolved, and whites are at the pinnacle—the most evolved. In short, he decided there is a black race and a white race and that blacks are lower beings, perhaps even in some ways less than human. Take a look at the charts and

---

21 Steven Rose. "Darwin, Race and Gender." *EMBO Reports*, Nature Publishing Group, April 2009, www.ncbi.nlm.nih.gov/pmc/articles/PMC2672903/.

diagrams that summarize Darwin's thought. You'll see that what I'm saying is true even if you haven't read what Darwin wrote.

By the way, you've probably heard that Darwin's famous book was titled *The Origin of Species.* Sounds innocent, doesn't it? The full title is *On the Origin of Species by Means of Natural Selection, or the Preservation of Favoured Races in the Struggle for Life.*

There it is. There's my objection. We all accept that human beings are higher life forms than, say, mice. No problem. That's not what Darwin's title refers to. He is talking about "Favored Races." Only human beings comprise the kind of "races" Darwin is talking about. He's saying in his title, at the very outset of his work, that some races—some types of human beings—are "favored" and some are not. Let's be more specific. Darwin taught that I am less evolved than my white neighbor.

Although best known for *On the Origin of Species,* Darwin does not specifically address the issue of race in this work. He merely lays the foundation for careless contemplation of it. It is in his 1871 book, *The Descent of Man,* that he shows his true colors. Here, his theories of natural selection reveal his white supremacist underpinnings.

Throughout the book, Darwin uses the word "savages" to describe seemingly every known ethnic group not of European descent. The use of the word "savage" was common among misinformed Europeans who believed other people's versions of civilization was beneath theirs.

It was meant to demean and devalue all of those it described. Darwin explained that the "highest races and the lowest savages" differ in "moral disposition ... and in intellect."[22] Continuing, Darwin says savages have, "low morality," "insufficient powers of reasoning," and

---

22 Charles Darwin, *The Descent of Man, and Selection in Relation to Sex, Volume 1* (New York: D. Appleton and Company, 1871). 34.

"weak power of self-command."[23] To top it off, Darwin's pen leaves no doubt as to how the application of survival of the fittest should be viewed amongst people groups. He says, "From the remotest times successful tribes have supplanted other tribes." And, he continues, "At the present day civilized nations are everywhere supplanting barbarous nations."[24]

So here we have an example of systemic racism. Darwin is taught as truth everywhere in America. Yet Darwin is racist. No question. Given that we live at a time when folks are taking down statues of Confederate generals out of a claim of racism, what should we do about Darwin? Wouldn't consistency prompt us to consider taking out of our textbooks the racist claims of one of the icons of the Western canon?

I know this will sound crazy to some folks. This is exactly how it sounds when anyone challenges the assumptions and practices of a racist system. *It's always been there. We've always done it this way. Why would we change?* These are the responses. Can you just imagine me marching up to the superintendent of public schools in my community and insisting that, as enlightened as they may be, that they are conducting a racist education program because Charles Darwin is at the core of the curriculum? That would hit the evening news, wouldn't it? And yet, it is undeniable.

Among the number of historical figures with whom I have serious issues, and Charles Darwin is near the top of that list. I think his system is a lie. I think his writings have been feeding systemic racism since *On the Origin of Species* was published in 1859. For more than a century and a half this man's philosophy has been shaping the world, encouraging a view of race that is little more than white supremacy codified.

---

23 Darwin, *The Descent of Man*, 93

24 Darwin, *The Descent of Man*, 154

It is true that to legitimize the broader theory of evolution, almost all proponents of Darwinism have distanced themselves from his racist intent. Still, ignoring a primary conclusion to his theory does not reduce its effect. The damage has been done. The die has been cast. Wittingly or unwittingly, modern day racist cultures owe much of their supportive thought to Mr. Darwin.

I'm required to pay taxes to support a public education system in which I'm encouraged to enroll my children. My seven kids, then, are expected to sit like good little boys and girls and learn Mr. Darwin's scientific theses. These ideas have woven in their premise that six of my children (I have one adopted white/asian daughter) are inferior to all whites. They are supposed to learn this, believe this, and, I assume, live this. Their academic progress is based upon them accepting this. Yet Darwinism is an enslaving lie when it comes to race and the status of people of varying skin colors.

The second area I have to explore with either individuals or organizations saying they want change is this: What is their real experience when it comes to people unlike them? In other words, what is their experience with reconciliation, with true ethnic unity and justice?

First let's define some terms. Justice is the finishing of a process that brings consequences to wrongdoers and equity to intentional imbalances. Reconciliation is the process of making peace between two opposing parties.

Reconciliation should not be confused with détente. Détente is just a cessation of conflict. It does not mean that real peace has been forged. It simply means that people aren't fighting anymore. Reconciliation has as its aim the bringing of substantive peace and harmony between enemies.

The simple truth is that most white folks think they are reconciled to blacks when they actually still have some distance to travel.
Their kids may have played with black kids. Their older children may
even have dated a black person. These kinds of interactive moments
can wrongly lead someone to conclude that they have fully bridged the
ethnic chasm, allowing them to declare that reconciliation has been
accomplished. While I deeply admire the progress they have made, they
have yet to arrive at the destination.

The beginning of true understanding, and thus reconciliation, is
realizing that the white experience and the black experience are not
identical, that they are not of the same kind. Without this recognition,
there can be no true reconciliation. It really is much the same when two
people are considering getting married. You have to go beyond admir-
ing the outer person and enjoying light interactions. You want to know
them—deeply. You want to know their history, what has hurt them,
what delights them, what they fear, how they feel in certain troubling
situations, what brings them comfort, and a thousand other insights
into how they are made and what life has done to them. To ignore these
things is to dismiss the real person in favor of a fantasy version of the
person. It is to enjoy them at a surface level but never love all that they
truly are inside. So it is with racial reconciliation and ethnic harmony.

You see, since white people are the dominant population in
American society, they have exercised their power to adjust the culture to their comfort level. This is what all dominant populations have
done throughout history. Yet in so doing, those in charge rarely think
about the comfort of those who aren't in charge. It's like an unaware
person adjusting the thermostat in a house to their own preference but
never thinking about the other people who live there. This is, however

unintentionally, what has happened in American society. It is a reality that is not lost on African Americans.

I have to say that the reason most whites don't recognize this dynamic is that often their black friends don't speak up. Let me explain this. Picture this conversation with me. A white man is talking to his black friend. He says that he saw a person on a dark street wearing a hoodie and was really afraid. Well, the black person has learned to be guarded, to never say fully what's on his mind. What he is thinking at that moment is, "So? What's there to be afraid of about a man with a hoodie?" You see, the simple matter of a hoodie is perceived by black and white in American society completely differently. And the difference in perception has to do with ethnicity and culture.

Let me tell you another hoodie story to make the point. It is not uncommon for football and basketball environments to set a dress code when its players are in the training facility, and for game day travel. Generally, the coach is the one who sets the clothing standard. Most coaches are white and most players are black. Years ago, I was told by a player from another team that a coach announced to his players that there would be no wearing of hoodies that cover the head in the team's facilities. He complained that he couldn't see a man's face when he wore a hoodie, that it might be a security issue too, and that he didn't want them worn on the grounds.

Well, the African American players took umbrage. They felt that the coach was being culturally, and by extension, racially insensitive. They said blacks don't wear hoodies to hide or because they have criminal intent. They wear them because hoodies are stylish and cool. They noted that few if any of the white players wear hoodies and thus this restriction carried with it the unintended consequence of feeling racist.

It was tense for a while because coaches are not accustomed to players dictating to them, but this coach finally relented.

Let's stay on this story for a moment. What was the true problem? It was that the white coach did not understand the black perspective. He had taken no time to see life through the eyes of his African American players. He just decided to adjust the cultural thermostat to his comfort level. He didn't know that his decision had anything to do with race. But it did, and considering that most of his players were African American, he should have educated himself on the individual he was hiring, and the subculture he was creating by hiring multiple players of the same hue. He needed to have taken a moment to consider how folks other than himself might be affected. This is part of what it means to seek reconciliation. You have to realize that your experience is not the only experience, your comfort and preferences are not all that exist, and so you have to slow down a bit and consider everyone in the room. If these kinds of measures are not employed, the unseen and unspoken conflict that lies just below the surface of our cross-cultural relationships will break through the veil of politeness and hit us squarely between the eyes.

I'm talking about hoodies here, but they aren't really the issue, of course. The real issues are a thousand other matters that are perceived completely differently by black and white, brown and yellow, red and any other skin color. The most productive levels of reconciliation require an adaptation that allows one to see through another's eyes. It requires us learning to feel from inside another's skin, if we can.

Let me use another example. I am the chaplain of the Washington Redskins. Except, I'm not. There is no NFL team called by that name any more. True, this word has been used for decades as the name of the Washington team. People—me included—used the name without any image forming in our minds except for a football team in the nation's capital. You see, the team was named by white people and I am a black man. So the offense of this word did not dawn on us until our Native American friends told us how this sounded to their ears.

To many of them, this word means approximately what "darky" might mean to me. It is even more offensive to them, though, since the word was often used in association with the practice of scalping Native Americans in the Old West. A quote from a Minnesota newspaper in 1863, the *Daily Republican*, shows this is true: "The state reward for dead Indians has been increased to $200 for every red-skin sent to Purgatory. This sum is more than the dead bodies of all the Indians east of the Red River are worth."[25] Only the most calloused heart could read these words and not understand why the several million Native Americans in our country would like for us to avoid that word. And we should, if we hope to be a compassionate, caring, reconciled people who have put their racist past behind them.

I should say also that sometimes attempts to address racist language and practices can end up going wrong even with the best of motives. A football coach I know (not with the Washington Football Team), issued an absolute ban on the "n-word" anywhere in the team's facilities. He thought he was doing something valiant that his black players would applaud. Instead, they stood up and said, "Wait a minute. You've just banned 90 percent of the music we listen to and also much of the way we talk to our black friends. We don't want you using that word, but don't stop us from using it. That cuts across our culture." Understand, any ethnic group has the right to use whatever language it wants for itself. So, when black people use the "n-word" to address one

---

25 Ian Shapira, "A brief history of the word 'redskin' and how it became a source of controversy," *The Washington Post*, May 19, 2016.

another, it is used to reduce relational distance and promote familiarity, while emptying the word of its pejorative punch.

Now, this coach's heart was in the right place but he made the same mistake that most whites make when it comes to trying to reconcile. He acted based on his own understanding, how the world looks from inside his skin, within his experience, and through his eyes. The wiser path would have been to talk to his African American players, the very people he was trying to serve, and find out how they viewed the "n-word." That would have allowed a discussion with the team that led to understanding, that banned the word for some and not for others, and that likely would have led to real reconciliation.

My point, then, is that when I'm helping a person or organization step toward building new history concerning race and ethnicity, my aim is to help them explore what their experience really is, how reconciled they truly are, and how free of bias they have become. A white man having lunch with a black man isn't reconciliation. A white family feeling progressive because their daughter had one date with a black young man isn't reconciliation either. No, what leads to reconciliation is starting to understand the way that black family sees the world. Why do they think of the police differently? Or hoodies? Or blackface? Or a traffic stop? What does it really mean to be included in the local high school or church or neighborhood? What is it like for them? This is where the beginning begins.

The next issue I raise with individuals and organizations who say they want change is one of the most important. Confronting this issue is essential, because it really will determine success or failure. It is the matter of the price.

We can't hide from the full weight of this. True racial reconciliation is expensive. I'm not primarily speaking in financial terms here, though reconciliation may ultimately include a monetary cost. I'm mainly speaking of the cost to what we hold dear about our culture, our traditions, our usual way of doing business. Hear me: change means change, not window dressing—and true change of the kind we are talking about is expensive.

The best way for me to illustrate this matter of cost is to use the example of churches. Though I work with organizations that range from law enforcement to athletic environments in promoting social justice and reconciliation, my years of leading churches will probably give us the most accessible, most easily understandable field for describing the cost of true change.

Over the past three decades, by God's grace, I have been privileged to build a truly multiethnic church in Chantilly, Virginia. I've already told you how that church began. Let me now tell you a bit about how we have sustained our structure, our mission and our vision. Doing so will help you understand some of the conversations I'm about to describe.

Our church numbers in the thousands and has scores of nationalities represented. The majority of the folks who attend are black, and represent many different nations. A large portion are also white, Asian, Latinx, and Arab. We are more a movement than a church in our thinking, and so we have planted churches beyond the mothership in Chantilly as far away as Vietnam, Los Angeles, Denver, Orlando, and Myrtle Beach. In our area we have congregations in downtown Washington, DC; Sterling, Virginia; and in Charlottesville, Virginia. In addition, we have Latinx and Korean congregations that meet in our building, both of whose pastors are on our church staff and minister to their congregations in their native language.

What is important for our topic here is that you understand how we build culturally. I am intent on having churches that reflect heaven, that are modeled on the kingdom of God rather than any one culture. So, we do not do worship that could be defined best by the white culture or that which could be defined by the black culture. I love them both, and they both find their legitimacy in God, but I'm building something different. We engage in as close to a multiethnic, kingdom type of worship as we can.

When you visit our church, you will likely be led by a worship team that can have as many as five or six ethnicities represented. This is intentional. We human beings tend to become what we behold. If I want to build according to the architectural model of the multiethnic expression, I have to reflect that intent in every aspect of our presentation.

I have also adjusted my preaching style to fit this vision. People might have expectations of my style, given that I'm a black pastor preaching to a church right on the edge of majority black Washington, DC. Again, though, I'm trying to build something specific and build intentionally. So, I sit on a stool at the front of the stage. I usually never stand and walk around unless I'm illustrating something. I'm passionate. I'm fiery at times. I more often sound like a motivational coach than a minister. I work to adapt my style to the people I am trying to reach. I do my best to speak from scripture, and keep the focus on Jesus.

I also let the kingdom model guide me in hiring. Our staff meetings look like a gathering that represents the diversity for which I am striving. We reflect the makeup of the church, which in turn hopefully reflects the makeup of the kingdom of God. If you come to Grace Covenant, I might be speaking or it might be an older white man on our staff, or a younger black woman or one of our Latinx pastors or perhaps one of our Korean pastors. And so it goes. Our guest speakers are generally equally as diverse.

It is the same with our volunteers. Your children might be taught by a grand Nigerian woman, an Asian children's pastor, or a young white man with a deep Virginia accent. As you enter the church you might be greeted by an Eastern or Western European, a woman from Ghana in colorful dress, or a young African American sporting creative tattoos welcoming you as he directs you to the information desk.

My role is not just pastor, but also Chief Kingdom Culture Officer. I have to teach. I have to coach. I often have to correct. This is simply to keep our culture right. If my message on a given Sunday service was too monoethnic, I will listen to it and adjust accordingly. If our worship in song doesn't quite hit the right "note" with respect to the style of song or lyrical content, we talk about it. I teach a bit. We make a change. If one of our many pastors says something in a sermon that could have been better said given our context. I will approach them after the first service so they can adjust for the next. Everyone on our staff is eager to be a culture keeper, everyone has the same kingdom vision.

Secondly, although I am amplifying the strengths and the victories that God has wrought through our service, I am not implying that we are a model church. Without question we are a work in progress. One wouldn't need to hang around us very long to see why there's no way we could ever be confused with perfection.

It has not been easy. We have made mistakes. We have had conflicts. People have left because they did not get what we are doing. They wanted what they had before. We were doing something strange to them. Nearly everyone who comes to our church—if they have been involved in churches before—has to let go of something they liked about a church that was built for people like them. Our church isn't white. It isn't black. It isn't any single culture. Everyone gives something up, and everyone who does gains even more. But there is a price for each person who joins our family. That's simply what kingdom life demands.

Now, I say all this by way of discussing the cost. Because God has done a unique work in the church I lead, I often have pastors come to me eager to have the same dynamics we have. I recall that one black pastor who was pastoring a strongly monocultural, traditional black church came to me and said excitedly, "I want what you've got! How do I get it?" The good news is that this man was seeing the kingdom through a fresh set of lenses and hungering for it. The challenging news for him was that I had grown our church this way from the beginning, but in order to have what we have he was going to have to change a church culture that already existed.

So, I was compassionately honest with him. I told him that he really didn't know that for which he was asking. I said, "You've got 3,000 three thousand people. If you're coming my way, it is most likely going to cost you half your church. You'll have to have non-blacks on your staff. You will have to change the way you perform worship in song, your preaching style, your children's church curriculum, and just about everything else you do." I told him his leadership style would have to change, and the members who were leaders would need to embrace and become welcomers of diversity. He would no longer be able to have a choir director conducting worship, and that the strongly monocultural Hammond B3 organ could only be used as a background instrument, if at all. New songs, new sound, new style, a new way.

"That's not all," I told him. "You should start praying with the white Presbyterian pastor down the street. Then, have joint services with him. Teach your people to surrender their style a bit in order to accommodate other believers, other traditions. It won't be easy, but this is how you get on the path to where we are and where we are heading."

Now, let's pause for a moment. I can imagine you, my reader, thinking that I was unusually frank with this pastor who was trying to do something good. And you are right. He was trying to do a noble and godly thing. Yet I would not have served him well if I had failed to tell him the truth of what it might all cost him. He had built a church with a traditionally black culture. It was a wonderful church. I love him and his congregation, and deeply admire how he has partnered with God to build something great. Yet I didn't want him sitting in his office dejected and feeling himself a failure a year later because he had less than half of the people he started with and most of his staff having resigned. I had to help him count the cost. He had to know what the price would be. He had to feel the weight of it before he even began.

Hear me: This is the way it is with all major moves toward true reconciliation. It means expensive change. It means sacrifice. It means extraordinary discomfort. We should know it, prepare for it, and understand it all as the necessary price of God's work on earth.

I've used a black pastor friend as my example here. Let me tell you what I often have to say to my white pastor friends. When something huge relating to race has happened in our world, white pastors often call me. I give them credit. They are often deeply disturbed and they say they want to make a difference. I'm glad. Each time I get a call like this, though, I find myself wishing that these pastors had built a partnership with me over time. We could have done so much good together and created something that would be a real bulwark in times of trouble. Instead, they have called in the middle of the crisis and asked what they can do. Bless them. They are coming late to the party but at least they are coming! I'm glad that they reached out to me, but it is hard to construct anything in a storm.

Who I have trouble working with effectively, though, are leaders who want to make a symbolic statement but do no lasting good. I'm sorry to say that many leaders think this way. They think in terms of ceremonies. They orient to pageantry and symbolism. This is fine, but when it is used as a substitute for meaningful cultural change, it falls woefully short. To them, image becomes more important than investment, the statement more important than social change. I encourage these leaders as best as I can by charting for them a path to real transformation. Sadly, they rarely take it. It is easier to accept the short quick fix that assuages guilt and fear without healing or reconciliation.

Let me keep using the example of church life and leadership. It is such a rich environment for exploring this matter of counting the cost of reconciliation that we are talking about.

Years ago, as our church was entering a phase of growth, I decided to start visiting churches around the United States where some measure of ethnic reconciliation was happening. It was quite an education. What I found was that there were many churches that defined themselves as multiethnic, with the vast majority of them being guided by white leadership. Only a few were stewarded by black leadership. Beyond the obvious fact that there are fewer black leaders available to lead (black folks only make up thirteen percent of the population), and therefore fewer multiethnic churches led by them, is the reality that it is harder for a white person to call a black leader his/her pastor than it is for a black person to call a white leader his/her pastor.

Most stores, businesses, schools, and organizations are controlled or owned by the dominant population. Today, we black folks rarely have to make an ethnic choice as to whether we are going to conduct business in these establishments because it is the air we breathe. It is the prevailing American cultural norm. We are used to it. Going to a pre-dominantly white church is akin to that.

Blacks becoming members of a white church is not significantly uncommon because we have already grown accustomed to the prevailing culture (when I say "easier" I do not mean easy). Yet, it rarely works in the reverse. Whites have a hard time becoming members of a traditionally black church. Why? Our culture is not the mainstream culture. White folks are less use to our mannerisms and idiosyncrasies. The whole experience is foreign to them. They might enjoy the visit, but to them it just doesn't feel like home. The pastor is likely to whoop or suddenly say "Ha!" in the middle of the sermon. A handkerchief makes a frequent appearance as the pastor gets increasingly ramped up while he or she is preaching. The choir sways. Music directors can be quite dramatic in their style of leading. Shouts of praise and extended "praise breaks" can happen at any moment. Then, of course, the service can easily run twice as long as the fifty-nine-minute dominant culture Sunday morning experience.

What I was interested in finding during my travels, then, was not just churches that had both blacks and whites, but churches that had a kingdom culture added to the recipe of multiethnic worship. In other words, had they created something new and reflecting heaven rather than just putting blacks in a white-cultured church or whites in a black-cultured church? My standard practice was to visit the church first and then sit with the pastor.

Remember that we are talking about counting the cost. Every pastor with whom I spoke said it was hard. They said there was more pain, texture, nuance, and entrenchment to both black culture and white culture than they ever knew. Many of them said true reconciliation was the hardest thing they ever attempted. I knew what they were talking about.

The differences in perspectives between black and white can often be found in nearly every aspect of a church's life.

Let's start with the fundamental matter of approach to God. Four hundred years of oppression—including two hundred and fifty years of slavery, one hundred years of Jim Crow laws, and the general intentional exclusion from the American dream—has inclined the African American's approach to God to be postured from a place of visceral need. Generally, we come to God beseeching him to deliver us from our difficulty. Our testimony is not unlike that of the psalmist when he says in Psalm 34:6, "This poor man cried, and the Lord heard him and saved him out of all of his troubles."

The white American church community, on the other hand, generally tends to approach God on the basis of want, directional guidance, forgiveness of wrong doing, and protection. If we were to highlight a scripture that exemplifies their approach to God, it might be Psalm 27:1–2, "The LORD is my light and my salvation; whom shall I fear? The LORD is the defense of my life; whom shall I dread? 2 When evildoers came upon me to devour my flesh, my adversaries and my enemies, they stumbled and fell."

Neither pathway exhaustively describes how either ethnic group approaches God, nor does every individual slot perfectly into these ethnic definers. Yet, those who well understand both cultures cannot on the whole dismiss these descriptions as inaccurate.

Black people carry pain with them every day. If not their own stemming from the personal mistreatment they have experienced while being black in America, then that of their ancestors, daily remembering the inherited stewardship by which they must faithfully grasp the opportunities wrought by blood.

Our pain is deep. Our pain is generational. So real is our pain, that if our community could be psychoanalyzed, we would most likely be found to be suffering from PTSD—post-traumatic stress disorder. Having this diagnosis does not imply that something is wrong with us, if wrong is defined as bad. It simply means that an issue which has been identified must be addressed.

Do Father's Matter? What Science Is Telling Us About The Parent We Overlooked, by Paul Raeburn is a well compiled series of studies that target fathers' contribution to procreation, and the corresponding health of their progeny. Countless studies have been done on the health of the mother as a relates to the condition of her ovum, prenatal care, and her child's well being after birth. Yet, few have been done evaluating the health of the father and how his mental and physical state affects his seed. Author Raeburn's book is a must read.

One of the highlights of the book is a study performed on male mice. "In a study presented at the Society for Neuroscience in November of 2013, and later published in **Nature,** Brian G. Dias and Kerry J. Ressler of Emory University in Atlanta reported that the fear produced by traumatic experiences can be passed on from males to their offspring" (Do Father's Matter, Chapter 1). To be true, there is a world of difference between mice and men, but the genetic similarities are so many that researchers have depended upon them to learn about us. In large part, their trust has been well founded.

Researchers placed male rodents in a confined environment while a specific aroma was piped into their space. In conjunction with the aroma, the researchers coordinated an electric shock to which the mice adversely responded. Repeatedly they combined these two stimuli in such a way that soon the mice would respond to the smell with great agitation even when no electric shock was present. Once the Pavlovian response was firmly embedded, they then paired the male mice with female counterparts. Weeks later, offspring were birthed. After some maturation, the offspring, like their fathers, were placed in a confined space. Researchers then introduced the exact aroma their male parents experienced before copulation. Surprisingly, the second generation mice responded with significant agitation to the smell. The effects of a previous generation's traumatic event had been passed down to the next, without having experienced the traumatic event themselves, nor having learned a behavior from their fathers. The inherited dysfunction was physiological and genetic.

The black man's four hundred year experience in America has been painful. Successive generations of trauma have conditioned us to be aware of the potential for danger; indeed, the smell of it. That said, I am not one to blame all my present day dysfunction on my ancestor's trauma. Still, I do not think it a stretch to conclude that generations of inhumane treatment endured by my forefathers might well have a negative genetic cascading effect on me.

I am convinced that this, along with the present day cultural challenges, strongly flavors our approach to God and church. It also should inform white people as to why we are more different from them than just skin tone might reveal. Yes, we all came from Adam. Yes, we all should believe and practice orthodox theology. But the branch of the Adamic family tree that produced the African American was often malnourished, damaged by the elements, and neglected. A good horticulturalist (leader) must take the time to study the branches that desire to be grafted into his spiritual vine so he will both know how to make them fruitful, and how they can grow both on and with the vine.

Most of the pastors I met with probably had no idea about these different approaches to God when they began the multiethnic congregational journey. Yet once the first step was taken, the price they had to pay was irrevocable, nonrefundable, and always increasing.

Let me take another example of what a reconciliation-oriented pastor has to manage. I often ask pastors how they handle troubling national events from the pulpit. A typical question might be, "How did you deal with the Trayvon Martin killing? Did you address it on Sunday morning?" Now, understand that I am asking black pastors this as well as white. I do this because it tells me a great deal about the culture of the church.

You see, I deal with nearly every nationally impacting event that has to do with race or social justice in our church's Sunday morning gatherings. I'm trying to build a kingdom people, a kingdom church. I have to guide them in the biblical response to what is happening around them. I have to point the way for our churches to make a difference. I cannot be fearful of offending or losing people. I have learned this reality to be as painful as it is inevitable.

My stewardship is first to my heavenly calling from God, second to the people he has called me to pastor, and third to the community He has called me to reach. These three are not in conflict. They work in harmonious synergy. Therefore, if God has called me to produce a multiethnic people for his glory, then what he's called me to produce must have relevance to those he has called me to reach. What I construct as a church ought to be relevant to my community, and habitable by my community. Therefore, if those who call us "home" choose to find another place to dwell because they are either offended by or intolerant of my biblical perspective on sociological issues, that is a clear sign that they have been with us as long as they needed to be.

If you choose to build a multiethnic church, and lead in a way that is culture-confronting, you will lose people and it will hurt. Still, you will gain far more as you construct the heaven-reflecting church you are called to build.

I should tell you, by the way, that when I deal with big issues during our services, no one is happy. This too is part of the price. Addressing sociological issues from a biblical hermeneutic pleases God more than it does anyone else.

You can imagine what upsets people. I was too sympathetic to whites. I was too empathetic to black folk. I was too hard on the police or not hard enough. I didn't fully explain the situation or I took sides or I missed the Lord on a certain point. People don't leave satisfied. They leave stirred up. None of this escapes me. I'm doing what I have to do to build a kingdom-minded people. And, yes, it's painful along the way—for us all!

Now it's time for this literary conversation to become even more uncomfortable. From this nation's inception, white folks prohibited us from worshipping with them. The unique flavor of our worshipping culture was birthed while bondage and oppression were everyday realities. The unintended benefit was we could express ourselves without restraint. True, there was the negro "spy" whose job it was to report to the master anything said or done that went cross-grain to the master's wishes. Even so, the church proved to be the one place where the black community could bring its corporate soul to God. Thus began the practice of black churches using the service of worship to coordinate sociological solutions to their oppressive circumstances, while crying out to God to right injustices and alleviate their pain.

The church was a haven for us. Indeed, a welcoming ship on troubled seas. Of course we talked about what the slave masters were planning. Of course we talked about Jim Crow and the death of Emmett Till and the Tulsa Riots and the Tuskegee Syphilis Experiment and what we'd heard about the Klan in our area and ten thousand other things that impacted us. We talked about all these and we prayed and we cried out to Jesus as a people who were helpless apart from God. There we found hope, support and strength as painful tales of injustice often became testimonies of victory by the hand of God.

The African American church talks about the world and how it is affecting them. The white church, not so much; the exception being discussions about national elections. I realize I am broad brushing both the African American and white church by categorizing in such narrow ways. But if I'm wrong to do so, I'm not all wrong.

Pastors tell me that they don't want to offend or that they don't know what to do because they have both Republicans and Democrats in their pews, or that the denomination hasn't taken a public stand or simply that they don't believe in a "political pulpit." I understand the stance on not being political. I stay away from politics as well, but that doesn't mean I stay away from culturally damaging moments, or sociological ills for which the broader community is required to repent.

Racism is wrong without it having a political overtone. Bigotry is wrong without it being colored by "red" or "blue." Some might choose to approach these matters from a political viewpoint, but not me. My responsibility is to disciple the sheep under my care by instructing them concerning the most accurate biblical response to the current crisis. Homiletically building this way enables the people under my care to better contextually address their sphere of influence with the Gospel message.

These differences between the white and the black church were illustrated to me time and again in my travels. I pondered them and talked them over with pastor friends around the country. I came to some important conclusions that, in the end, were surprisingly encouraging to me. My first conclusion was that it is normative for a multiethnic church to have blacks in it who are accommodating the dominant culture just as they do in the broader society. To the leadership of those congregations, I tip my hat. I applaud them for moving beyond their comfort zones to embrace "different." Could they more deeply explore what reconciliation means on a level that would afford them a greater depth of unity? Without question! Still, I am never mad about anything that is progressing. Good work!

My second conclusion is that black church culture can exist with white folks involved, but generally this happens in much smaller percentages than the other way around. To the white people who have joined black churches, let me say, "thank you." You stepped over a threshold, to participate in a world that is filled with people who are not like you. Your courage is commendable!

Having said this, please understand that what these whites have done does not make them better Christians than those who have not made that choice. I repeat, white people who have chosen to call a black house of worship their home are not better Christians because they chose to go to a church filled with people who are not like them. Yet one fact is undeniable. By "baptizing" themselves in an unfamiliar culture, they have enriched their lives in ways that never would've occurred if they had remained in the culture to which they were born. To be sure, they are farther down the road of reconciliation than most in the dominant culture.

Moving now from the white member to the black government of the church, what responsibility does the leadership of a black church have to intentionally incorporate the unique elements of white culture? Well, if they want to travel the road that leads to the fullest reconciliation possible, a lot! However, this must be said again: There exists no biblical mandate stating that Christian congregations must be multieth-nic. Thus, if a black church wants to stay ethnically and culturally black, that's fine. If a white church wants to stay ethnically and culturally white, that's fine. Churches are not demoted to second class citizenry in the kingdom of God if they do not travel this road.

The first church in Jerusalem was made up of strictly Jewish con-verts (some Hellenistic and some Israel natives, but overwhelming Jewish by birth). Knowing their profound impact on the progress of the Gospel, none would be justified to criticize them for their homogeneity. Having said that, what is problematic is choosing to be ethnically sep-arate even when opportunities to connect are available. What I mean is that though we are not mandated to be congregationally multiethnic in our Sunday worship every week, we are called to love and preserve unity with the whole Church.[26] To do this is to recognize the Church of which every church is a part, confirming and preserving the unity that God has granted. These are done best when we pursue relationship— pastors of black churches connecting with pastors of white churches. White and black church pastors choreographing moments when their congregations can meet together, for worship or events.

Finally, I realized something that was troubling but that brought a measure of understanding to my heart. The simple fact is that there are very few churches in the United States that are experiencing the richness of diversity (beyond ethnically diverse window dressing) that biblical reconciliation provides. Sadly, my count is under one hundred. I'm sure there are more of which I am not aware, but that I went looking for them and could only find a small percentage says volumes.

I understand why there are not more. I really do. It is just flat hard to plan, architect, execute, and build a reconciled multiethnic

---

26 Ephesians 4:3b–4 NASB

people. For most pastors, it seems to be duty enough just to faithfully participate in the unending struggle of building a normal homogeneous church. Why complicate the already impossible by intentionally adding a multiethnic pile on to the architectural design? In so doing, one has only made more work for oneself! Yet, by doing so, skills develop within the church that help the broader community discover the answers to the ethnic tensions they face. The church gradually becomes the witness of Christ to the community.

So I felt a degree of peace when I was done with my search. I thought I would find churches that were miles ahead of where we were in true reconciliation. Sadly I didn't. I found pastors trying but weary from the struggle. I found churches that reached out and loved those unlike them but who had not achieved as much reconciliation as they had hoped. And I found a few, just a few, that had started to do that very hard thing: build a church with a culture that looked like the throne room of heaven in matters of race and ethnicity.

Although I continually find myself troubled by what wasn't happening in our nation, my findings in the church brought me a bit more peace knowing that pastors were genuinely trying to become more than they were.

Again, what I was hoping to find was something that happened so rarely there was hardly language to describe it. In fact, I often used an illustration from music that helped me make the point.

To understand this illustration you have to know that in the town of my birth, Kansas City, Kansas, the radio dial has for years represented the distinction between whites and blacks when it comes to music and radio show tastes. When I was growing up, African Americans for the most part listened to the stations above 101 on the radio dial. That's where my people's programming was. Whites, of course, lived below 101, from 87–100 on the radio dial.

This is even true of religious music. Gospel generally lives above 101. Contemporary Christian generally lives below 101. To say it another way, the left side is white, the right side is black. And it has been this way for years. If I wanted to listen to Gospel music, I went right. If I wanted to sneak over and listen to contemporary Christian, south of 101 I went. They were separate experiences tied to a separate sound and never did the two meet.

Then came my dear friend Israel Houghton. I hope you recognize his name. Starting in the late 1990s, he pioneered a whole new sound of Christian worship music, creating something I had never heard before. He blended R & B, Gospel, and Contemporary Christian music. Chord progressions that defined black gospel were combined with lyrics that went both ways and instrumentation that had a distinct contemporary Christian feel. His sound was fresh, neat. Before long, both black and white believers started joining in on his type of music. The truth is that Israel had created a new style of music. It was hugely popular, largely because it reached beyond the old categories. It tore down walls. It called blacks and whites to each other.

When I heard it, I knew that this type of worship fit the theology that God had produced in me. I didn't always have words for what I wanted to build, but I heard it declared in Israel's music. I didn't want a black church with whites folded into it or a white church with blacks making do. I wanted something new—a new culture, a new expression, a new unity, and way of reaching the world. In short, I wanted church made new, made heavenly, made revolutionary.

Here is the most important point. I didn't just *want* church made new, I had to have it. Nothing else would do. I wasn't called to anything else, wasn't made for anything else, no matter the price. I would learn over time that the price was dear. This was a cross I was called to bear, and because I had already "died," and my life was "hidden with Christ in God,"[27] I was fine. Cost me what it will, I had to have a piece of the heavenly on earth.

Now you know why I stress this matter of cost so much and why I have taken so many pages to describe it here. If you choose to build multiethnically, you will not erect anything that challenges America's cultural storms if your aim is to make a short-term statement. You will not change the world with mere symbols, pageantry and window dressing. You have to do the hard thing of remaking what you have before you can realize the transformation you want to see. It will be one of the hardest things you have ever done, but it is worth it to know that you were able to be small part of the answer to Christ's instructional prayer, "Thy will be done in earth, as *it is* in heaven."[28]

Thus far in this chapter, I've emphasized cultures, largely church cultures, and what they produce when it comes to reconciliation. I did this on purpose. I wanted you to see that reconciliation is a matter of giving up that which is comfortable in favor of that which heals and reconciles us genuinely one to another. This is always a matter of culture, always a matter of understanding backgrounds, beliefs, and attachments to what we've known. Once you start working at this level, real change in the real world becomes possible.

Let me give you an example of how the right culture can lead to the right kind of transformation in the real world, so to speak—in business, sports, government, or any arena really.

---

27 Colossians 3:3 NASB
28 Matthew 6:10 KJV

A crisis occurred not long ago in a Chick-fil-A store in the Tidewater region of Virginia. It seems that an owner had just bought the franchise for one of the famous chicken restaurants in the area. It wasn't a new store, but one that already existed and already had a staff. After he made the purchase, the owner brought people with him from his other stores and put them in charge of the new store. In the process, some folks were demoted without salary loss. Among those who were demoted were two black women.

This didn't go well. The women charged discrimination, called in the NAACP, and started picketing the store. This completely stopped the drive-through, which, as you may know, is the lifeblood of a Chick-fil-A operation. The owner was going out of his mind because of loss of income and bad press.

It was at this time that the owner heard about Jared Green. Now, Jared is a young man who has grown up in my church. His father is the football star Darrell Green, who is so beloved in Washington, DC, that there is a highway named after him. He's one of the top one hundred NFL players of all time. For decades he has been a governmental leader in our church. Through the years, Jared has absorbed the culture of our church and lived out reconciliation in powerful and society-changing ways. I couldn't be prouder of him. He had recently started a company called *Engage365* to empower businesses to function optimally using biblical principles. He is good at what he does. Really good.

Jared has a unique gift for repairing just the kind of tense situations the Chick-fil-A owner was dealing with. When the man heard about Jared, he asked him to come and help. Jared agreed, and within thirty-six hours the NAACP, the city council, the CFA owner, and the aggrieved women were all brought to a place of peace. The owner apologized. Other steps were taken. The community won. And everyone called Jared a hero.

What had happened? The culture of our spiritual house landed on our troubled society and brought peace to troubled waters. This is why I have worked so hard to build our church on a different basis and to fine-tune our culture time and again. The church is meant to be whole in order to help the world. I've fought to have something on earth that looks like heaven because I want truth in my house so we can fix the world. It is harder. We grow slower. We deal with stuff no one wants to talk about on a Sunday. Some folks can't see their way to come with us. Okay. But at least we help them with what we tell them and model for them. Ultimately, we are about being God's healing answer for our embattled world.

So here's the lesson and the main theme of this chapter. Get your heart right, get your culture right, then you can take the steps needed to fix real world situations. Now comes the question: Where does a person from the dominant culture begin to start the process of reconciliation?

I want to suggest three simple statements that create a beginning in any attempt at reconciliation. Here they are:

I feel your pain.
I'm sorry.
How can I help?

To say you feel the pain of those who have been abused and oppressed, hated and denied justice is not to say you've had the same experience. It is simply to say that you can, as a human being, feel the horror and injustice of what they've been through. You likely felt this pain, whatever your color or ethnicity, when you read the chapter *The*

Press of the Past Upon Us in this book. You may be white or some other racial makeup, but perhaps you saw the broad sweep of antiblack racism in America in that chapter and you felt the pain of slavery and Tulsa and Tuskegee and George Floyd at least a bit, and you care now more than you did. This is all we are asking. You are in touch with our pain. You aren't defending. You aren't countering. You are just understanding and allowing yourself to feel it.

In the same way, to say you are sorry doesn't mean that you have engaged in mistreatment of a downtrodden people yourself. It simply means that you are sorry for what they have gone through. You feel it. You wish it hadn't happened. As a fellow human being you grieve what they have been through. You are sorry. You would say this if a friend broke an ankle, wouldn't you? You would say it if he came down with the flu, or if he lost a loved one. *I'm sorry you are sick, and I am sorry for your loss.* The apostle Paul empathized with the saints in the city of Corinth by saying, "Who is weak without my being weak? Who is led into sin without my intense concern?"[29] In his letter to the Romans, the apostle Paul encourages the saints to empathize with others in their congregation by writing, "Rejoice with those who rejoice, and weep with those who weep."[30] It is simple compassion and manners to feel sorry for someone who has been wronged. Sadly, the black community has too often wept alone.

Just after some of the horrible shootings in 2020, our church planned a racial reconciliation event on a local plantation. Hundreds of slaves had been kept at the plantation and we thought this would be a great place to repent for the sin of slavery and commit ourselves— white, black, Asian, Hispanic, Arab, Persian, you name it—to a greater

---

29 2 Corinthians 11:29 NASB

30 Romans 12:15 NASB

day of racial reconciliation. We thought the event might change some things not only in our minds but in the spiritual atmosphere of our region. I asked a local pastor of some prominence to join us.

Shockingly, he refused. He said, "I can't repent when I had nothing to do with the sin. I can't reach back and apologize for my ancestor's wrongs." I thought, "Wow, really?" I've listened to people bemoan the pain and abuse their father inflicted on them. As a father, in poxy I have expressed to them my sorrow for their dad's failure to steward the position God gave him. Empathy expressed in this way has never ceased to build a more effective onramp for God's healing. Nehemiah identified with the sins of his fathers and repented for them.[31] I've stood before God and repented for our nation's assault on the unborn. Never participated in an abortion." It's called identificational repentance. It means you acknowledge another's wrongdoing, identify with its wrongness and commit to correct its ill effects in your day. Yet this pastor wasn't having it. He couldn't bring himself to weep with us over the sins in our land, past and present. I was sad for him, very.

Finally, then, there is the all-important question: How can I help? I say it is all-important because this question shows that you are seeking information, asking the wronged to help you figure out how to address wrongs. It is a protection from any of us just barging in with a narrow understanding and assuming anything we do will make a difference. We have to ask. We have to probe a bit. We have to find our pain points and together find paths to healing.

Let me give you some examples. When Michael Brown was killed on the streets of Ferguson, Missouri, in 2014, local law enforcement in my area asked me to help them understand the black rage. I was proud of them for asking and happy to help.

---

31 Nehemiah 1:4–6

We held two forums, one with members of my church and the community and another with the NFL Washington Football Team players. At the community forum, there was great concern about the militarization of the police that had been demonstrated in Ferguson, where there had been souped up Humvees and vehicles with gun turrets on them. There had also been water cannons and weaponry that seemed more appropriate to a nation going to war. All of it was on American streets poised to be used against unarmed protestors.

One young man stood up and asked, "Why do the police have such military equipment? And are you authorized to use it?" The chief of police of Fairfax County, Ed Rossler, answered that the police in our area only had drones so far but not the kind of equipment used at Ferguson. Then the young man asked, "If we protested like they did at Ferguson, would we be met with this kind of militarized police response here?" The police chief, obviously deeply moved, was quiet for a moment and then said, "Never here." Let me tell you that his manner and that two word answer broke things open. The folks in that room heard each other out for another hour and a half. When it was all over, the 250 people in that room gave the police a standing ovation.

The forum with the football players took a different direction. The team members were eager to ask about profiling. They told stories of being stopped for "driving while black" and of being held by police for no more reason than how they looked. Some of these big, muscular NFL players began to cry as they told their stories. The police officers I had brought to the meeting were shaken. Frankly, few of them had any idea that players in the NFL, many of them well known and better off financially than most Americans, had endured such treatment. The police pledged in that forum to make a difference. They spoke of training differently. And they apologized for what these men had endured.

It was a healing moment and it all happened because the police came with a willingness to feel pain, apologize, and seek to make a difference.

Let's turn the focus on you. I've told stories in this chapter. I've been transparent in describing my interactions with others. Yet my reason for doing all this—in fact, saying everything that I've said in this book—is to ignite a fire in you.

I want to ask you now to survey your soul. Why are you reading this book? Have you told people you want to help create change? If you want to be part of a trendy, socially relevant crowd or if you simply want to make a short term "statement," be careful about stepping onto the battlefield of social change and peacemaking. You will have to fight harder than you thought for a win that has more reward in heaven than you may experience here. However, if you really want to be an agent of substantive change, and you want from your core to help turn the direction of the cultures you are part of and of our broader society too, then I welcome you. Jump in.

As you jump in, take stock of your prior experience. What has your culture been? What has shaped you? What has made you who you are? Look deeply into yourself and answer these questions. Look deeply also into the cultures that you are part of—your school, your business, your city, your family, and any others. Know yourself. Be certain of what is launching you as you step out to make a difference.

Just as important, count the cost. Though our efforts at social change are perhaps a bit easier because of some of the awakening that is happening in our current society, we are still battling attitudes, practices, and cultures that are centuries old. It won't be easy. I don't want you to start and then quit. I also don't want you to fail, wounded and disillusioned. I want you to succeed. So, count the price to you and to all you lead in declaring yourself for change.

Then, finally, remember those three simple phrases that have the power to change everything.

I feel your pain.

I'm sorry.

How can I help?

If you can bring yourself to turn to people unlike yourself, people whom society has knocked down, both in history and today, and you can say these three things as an informed, sincere, willing person, then change can begin with you. In fact, you can lead in the changes you've dreamed might happen in society.

Now, do one additional thing. If you choose to travel this road of reconciliation to its end, I urge you to kneel before God, the maker of heaven and earth, and ask for his grace, his power, and his wisdom. Tell him you want to glorify him in all that you are about to do, and that you understand that this is his holy cause, his eternal purpose to make heaven happen on earth. Take some time with this. Sit still in his presence. Let these moments be like a commissioning. Do this so sincerely that you will always remember this moment—in the good times and the bad, in the defeats and the victories—and you will always see it as the moment that sent you into this great battle for love in our world.

CHAPTER 6

A LETTER TO
YOUNG BLACK AMERICA

My Dear Young Friends,

These words likely come to you as the world seems to be swirling around you and your soul is in turmoil. You've seen people who look like you killed and in the most heartless ways. You've heard your people group vilified in your nation's politics. You've seen some in your ethnic group rise to heroic heights and others reflect the worst of human nature. You have questions. You have fears. You long to make a difference. You want to be the change.

I understand.

I want to speak to you in this letter as a father. I mean this both in the sense that I am likely older than you and also in the sense that I have been serving our cause far longer than you. Allow me to offer some wisdom, some perspective, that may make your journey and your contending more effective, more transforming, and perhaps more of a joy.

Our journey, the struggle for black equality in America, has been marked by acts of heroism, legal genius, empathetic deeds from noble abolitionists, and, certainly, inhumane resistance from the dominant population. At each significant moment, there was opportunity for the black man to either settle for the meager progress that had been made or perhaps to quit when the blowback became too much to bear. Fortunately, neither of these options were chosen by those who came before us in our struggle.

Yet there is a truth we often forget about those who have fought for freedom. Many of them were young, perhaps even younger than you are. Phillis Wheatley was twenty when she was first published. Frederick Douglass was also twenty when he escaped to freedom. Sojourner Truth was twenty-nine when she escaped and Harriet Tubman was twenty-seven.

Similarly, in the 1960s, the "Greensboro Sit-Ins" were coordinated by four students—Ezell Blair Jr., Franklin McCain, Joseph McNeil, and David Richmond—who were later nicknamed the "Greensboro Four." They were just freshmen at North Carolina A&T University.

When I think of the young blacks who have fought for us so valiantly, I'm reminded that the use of the young in a righteous cause is not new. Long ago, Jesus of Nazareth employed this strategy when selecting his disciples.

Christ was the wisest man who ever drew breath. In his day, the thinking about age and leadership was much as it is today: if you want religious service done well, find the most experienced, eloquent, and capable ministers to carry your message. Jesus broke from that tradition.

It is widely thought that he selected twelve inexperienced young men whom none thought equal to the task. Peter was the elder who was probably in his thirties, and John was likely no more than a teenager. Christ chose youth over maturity, penitence over experience, and hope over certification. He believed in young people.

Those who followed Christ also followed his example. The apostle Paul, the author of two-thirds of the New Testament, made it his practice to find young people in whom he could invest his ministry. Tradition has it that Timothy was about sixteen years old when Paul visited his home at Lystra.[32] That visit culminated in Timothy being selected as a member of Paul's ministry team. Their relationship grew so close that Timothy became a man Paul addressed as "my son."[33] Titus, another disciple of Christ who was on Paul's team, was also young enough to be referred to by Paul as his "child in the faith" (Titus 1:4).

Other great struggles in the world have followed this example. With unsurpassed vision, energy, and a belief that obstacles are disguised opportunities, young Chinese voices were heard around the world from Beijing's Tiananmen Square in 1989. Rowena He, an assistant professor at St. Michael's College in Vermont, was a participant in the Tiananmen Square push for democracy. He was part of the movement that engulfed China as youth demanded democratic reforms and economic freedoms, and later the author of *Tiananmen Exiles: Voices of the Struggle for Democracy in China.* In an interview with *National Geographic,* he says, "I envy the freedom that my students enjoy here ... When I was around their age, millions of us took to the streets in cities throughout

---

32 Acts 16:1–3

33 1 Cor 4:17; 1 Tim 1:18; 2 Tim 1:2

my home country demanding these basic rights that American students receive as their birthright and often take for granted."[34]

In the same way, the Middle East's Arab Spring was sparked in 2010 by masses of young people rebelling against government corruption, human rights violations, impoverishing economic policies, and law enforcement abuse. By the thousands, they rallied and protested after a young street vendor set himself on fire when police confiscated his vending cart. Although older generations also participated in this unprecedented demand for change, analysts like M. Chloe Mulderig of Boston University believes that the Arab Spring "could not have occurred without the ideological and numerical push of a huge mass of angry youth."[35]

In 2018, tens of thousands of American junior high and high school students coordinated a walkout from their classrooms in support of the seventeen students murdered at Marjory Stoneman Douglas High School in Parkland, Florida.[36] Their objective was to show that their voices could be heard as effectively as the voices of adults. Indeed, they were! Parkland, Florida, students, in addition to their walkout, also began asking partner companies of the National Rifle Association to sever ties with the organization. The result? In the following days, over a dozen companies canceled their support for the NRA.[37]

---

34 Erin Blakemore, "Youth in Revolt: Five Powerful Movements Fueled by Young Activists," *National Geographic,* March 23, 2018. https://www.nationalgeographic.com/news/2018/03/youth-activism-young-protesters-historic-movements/#close.

35 Erin Blakemore, "Youth in Revolt: Five Powerful Movements Fueled by Young Activists."

36 Sarah Gray, "What to Know About March for Our Lives and Other Student-Led Gun Control Protests" March 12, 2018, Time. https://time.com/5165794/student-protests-walkouts-florida-school-shooting/.

37 Jackie Wattles, "More than a dozen businesses ran away from the NRA. How it went down." February 26, 2018, CNN. https://money.cnn.com/2018/02/25/news/companies/companies-abandoning-nra-list/index.html.

What is my point in citing all of this productive and nonviolent social change engineered by the young? It is to encourage you. It is to motivate you. You are not on the sidelines of this generation longing for a day of impact. You are leaders, change agents, social reformers— NOW! I want you to see this and believe it as much as any other truth I have to share in this book.

The young often do not recognize the power they have. This is both because the older generation speaks down to them—telling them to wait until they are ready and not to think too highly of themselves— and because of the natural insecurity of young people. The young know they aren't quite ready. They know they don't have the degrees and the experience and perhaps the resources they need. Yet most of the change we need in our society is exactly the kind young people can create. It is a cry of conscience. It is an example of kindness and care. It is the energy to champion a cause even if that championing isn't quite as sleek and organized as older folks might want it to be. Hear me. There is no perfect age. There is no ideal time. Do right when you can do it. Be respectful and don't give in to violence and hate. But do what you can when you can with all that you can. This is how you change your world. Our headlines are confirming every day that mere children are changing the world. I don't want you to let your innate insecurity or messages from adults or simple fear to keep you from your youthful moment of impact. The need is too great, and you are far more powerful than you have ever dreamed.

I also want to challenge you about another matter. It is easy for those who have been mistreated to shrink back in bitterness and stand apart from the society that has wronged them. All of us who live in black skin understand the insults, feel the blows, have absorbed the hatred and the injustice. I have experienced all of this too. Yet I want to urge you not to retreat, not to separate, not to pull back from the good you are called to do because of offense. Be aggressive in learning to forgive. Don't let other's misguided actions be the compass for your response. Do better than the bad done to you.

We are at our best when we are not retreating in anger but investing our gifts for the good of others. This is what we are made for. This is what changes lives. This is how we fulfill our destinies. This is also what the great chronicle of black America illustrates for us. This is the inheritance we are called to steward, and how we fashion change in our time.

Phillis Wheatley heard that voice of freedom as she penned her poems. They inspired all who read them, including George Washington, the father of our country. Consider just one account of this dramatic episode in our history:

> In December of 1775, Washington—the newly appointed
> Commander-in-Chief of the Continental Army—received a letter
> from Wheatley containing an ode written in his honor. The poem
> illustrates Wheatley's somewhat surprisingly passionate patriotic
> sentiment, which factors strongly in much of her poetry. It ends
> with a stanza reading:

Proceed, great chief, with virtue on thy side,
Thy ev'ry action let the goddess guide.
A crown, a mansion, and a throne that shine,
With gold unfading, WASHINGTON! Be thine.

> Washington responded with a letter expressing his appreciation
> for Wheatley's poem. He even considered publishing it but feared
> people might interpret that action as self-aggrandizing. Not only
> was this letter the only one Washington is known to have written

to a former slave, but he addressed Wheatley as "Miss Phillis" and signed off as "Your obed[ien]t humble servant," unusual and even paradoxical courtesies. Washington also extended an invitation for Wheatley to call on him at his headquarters in Cambridge, Massachusetts.[38]

Three months after the "shot heard round the world" was fired in Lexington, Massachusetts, this former slave—and not yet American—inspired the man who was the greatest hero in our nation at the time. Her work was not only favorably received by this great man, but also commended. It might be a bridge too far to claim that Miss Wheatley's encouragement motivated the general of the Continental Army to victory. Still, it is wise to never underestimate the value of inspirational words. We should strive to live in the power of the same motivation.

In addition to the black heroes and heroines, there were many young white people who publicly denounced racism. One of them was Anthony Benezet. In 1731, at eighteen years of age, Anthony Benezet became one of the earliest American abolitionists. In 1775, he helped organize the first antislavery society: The Society for Relief of Free Negros Unlawfully Held in Bondage. After Benezet's death, his work lived on when Benjamin Franklin and Dr. Benjamin Rush reorganized the group to be named The Pennsylvania Society for Promoting the Abolition of Slavery.

Harriet Tubman, best known for her skills in designing and leading the "underground railroad"—the pathway north for escaped slaves, dotted by sanctuary homes owned by sympathetic abolitionists—fought in the Civil War, and was the first woman in American history ever

38 Heartman, Charles Frederick. *Phillis Wheatley (Phillis Peters): A Critical Attempt and a Bibliography of Her Writings.* United States: For the author, 1915. 19–22.

to lead a military regiment into battle.[39] Sojourner Truth was another leader in the abolitionist cause and was celebrated as an was an outstanding public speaker. She fought hard for women to enjoy the same rights as privileged American men. In 1828, the year after the slave trade was abolished in New York, she became one of the first blacks to win a legal case against a white man. She sued her former master, winning the right to reclaim her son. She fought for what was right knowing that it would also lift others up.

Frederick Douglass escaped his physical bonds, educated himself, and became one of the finest orators in American history. He wrote at least five books, the most famous of which was, *My Bondage, My Freedom*. He also published a newspaper, *The North Star*, which detailed the black man's struggle and the disparities between the lives of white Americans and those of the enslaved. During the Civil War, he conferred with President Abraham Lincoln concerning the treatment of black soldiers. After the Civil War, he advised President Andrew Johnson on the matter of black suffrage.[40]

In 1872, without his consent, Douglass became the first African American nominated for vice president of the United States. This was as Victoria Woodhull's running mate on the Equal Rights Party ticket. President Benjamin Harrison later appointed him the United States Minister Resident and Counsel General to Haiti. This was not bad at all for a man who at birth was valued just above his master's cow. He was a free and prosperous black man, but he could not rest until freedom and prosperity came for others of his race and of his time.

39 https://www.google.com/amp/s/api.nationalgeographic.com/distribution/public/amp/news/2016/04/160421-harriet-tubman-20-dollar-bill-union-spy-history

40 William McFeely, *Frederick Douglas* (New York: W.W. Norton, 1991), 227, 229.

Again, white people, too, served the cause. In 1939, Juliette Hampton Morgan—a fresh-out-of-college white public school teacher, a librarian in Montgomery's Carnegie Library, a soon-to-be director of research at the Montgomery Public Library, and an employee of a local bookstore—lost her job at her bookstore when she repeatedly wrote the local paper (*The Montgomery Advertiser*) denouncing the "back of the bus" policies forced on black riders in Montgomery, AL. She not only penned her displeasure, but became a thorn in the side of the entire Montgomery bus system. The website "Tolerance" states,

> *One morning as she rode the bus, Morgan watched a black woman pay her fare and then leave the front door of the bus to re-enter through the back door, as was the custom. As soon as the black woman stepped off, the white bus driver pulled away, leaving the woman behind even though she'd already paid her fare. Incensed, Morgan jumped up and pulled the emergency cord. She demanded the bus driver open the door and let the black woman come on board. No one on the bus, black or white, could believe what they were seeing. In the days that followed, Morgan pulled the emergency cord every time she witnessed such injustices.*

Shortly afterward, Tuskegee Airmen bravely engaged German aircraft during World War II so that white American bombardiers could drop their ordinance on Germany. In 1947, Jackie Robinson endured horrible insults from fans and opposing players to pave the way for other black ballplayers into the Major Leagues.

Martin Luther King Jr., of course, stands alone as the most important voice for equality in our era. At the age of twenty-six, he charted a path that would commend him as a pillar of justice, truth, and reconciliation. America can never do enough to honor his memory. Of course, there were other great heroes, and their names will ever be remembered, ever be celebrated as sacrificial warriors in a righteous cause.

Yet what is the lesson of all this for us? What are these legendary figures urging upon us now from the balcony of heaven? They are telling us that God has made us for more than bitterness or retreat. He has made us for a greater purpose than to answer abuse with abuse. Instead, we are made to invest our lives. We are called upon to use our gifts to lift those of every color and ethnicity, nationality and gender, to the heights for which they are made. This has been the greatness of generations past. And it can be the greatness of our generation if we will, as Abraham Lincoln urged us, allow the better angels of our nature to lift us to our best.

Now, my young heroes in the making, I want to say some things to you that are difficult to hear. I want you to consider that we have been entrusted by our ancestors with a great task in this generation. In fact, it is more than simply a trust of our forebearers, it is a divine calling. If we believe this and set ourselves to be commissioned by it, then I have to ask you a vital question: Have we set our purposes high enough?

We seek equality in our society and this is understandable. We yearn for what is ours as creations of God, as human beings, and citizens in an American society built upon rights and constitutional guarantees. For these rights we should never cease to strive. Yet we should know—in fact all should know—that granting black America these rights and also righting the scales of justice will mean some loss of privilege by the comfortable in society. It will mean some sacrifice. We cannot hide from this, nor should we.

Hear me, though. This is not socialism. Socialism is the belief that wealth should be apportioned by government in such a way that prosperity is equally diminished for all, equally held in check. This is an idea that we should resist. Americans have inscribed on their hearts far too much constitutional independence to become completely dependent upon society. We are reticent to put our trust in government as provider and arbiter. Instead, we advocate for a just society in which we care for those with less. We realize, of course, that this "care" burdens society with more than just legislative action. It requires sacrifice. It requires humility. It may require the relinquishing of privileges, particularly privileges gained at the expense of others. We understand that this is what is required in order to form "a more perfect Union."

This will not be easy. Rarely if ever in history has a dominant population intentionally reduced their standing in order to elevate those with less. Why? Because it feels like something is being taken from them in order to give to those who do not have. The privileged feel "Robin Hooded," and scream that an injustice is being done to them.

Frankly, many members of the dominant population would rather keep black folks in a state of despair than sacrifice a layer or two of privilege. This is why there is such outrage against affirmative action and cries of injustice when reparations are suggested to address prior injustices, or when admissions standards are adjusted to allow blacks a few favored seats at a prized educational institution.

The simple truth is that those who have status wish to keep it. White folks don't want to hear that, but since they are the beneficiaries of their ancestor's mistreatment of blacks, it is only right for the equality conversation to start there. They claim reverse racism. They insist that nothing is owed the blacks of this generation to address injustices of two centuries ago. Even for those who grudgingly assent to the rightness of the claim, the relational, emotional, and sociological mountain just seems too high to climb.

With this being said, then, let us think a bit differently about our efforts to balance the scales of injustice on an ethnic basis. Let us consider an approach that will not reduce our press for equality, but accomplish far more than mere equality. The approach I'm talking about is reconciliation.

Earlier we examined the notion of reconciliation in the context of church integration and relational understanding, but the concept of reconciliation goes much deeper than just developing techniques that aid inclusiveness. It is unique among relational and sociological solutions. This is because it requires a degree of sacrifice, of surrendering self-interest—on both sides. When reconciliation does its best work it is empowered by the strongest force known to man: love.

In true reconciliation, the offended pursues the offender even if the offender is uninterested or antagonistic. The injured cares even for those who have done harm, is willing to never be made whole personally if it means that a friend can be made from an enemy, an advocate from an adversary.

In the same way, the offender is responsible to cease his injurious acts, to apologize for wrongful deeds, and to make amends for opportunities lost, pain caused, and possessions stolen. Upon both the wrongdoer and the wronged, reconciliation places expectations, but not demands. It will not force either party to place flesh on its bones.

Now, the English word "love" is unusual because its meaning is always determined by the context in which it is used. We "love" our friend, "love" ice cream, "love" our spouse, and "love" God using the same word in each case. And we think we know what is intended. Still, without more exact words to use for "love," we are left to our own interpretation as to what the user means when they say "love."

The ancient Greeks did not have this problem. They developed four words to describe the multifaceted concept of love: *phileo, storge, eros,* and *agape.* We would benefit by understanding the more precise meanings of these four words.

The word *phileo* (fill-EH-oh) refers to brotherly love. This is the love we feel for our fellow man, the goodwill and affection we intend for all people. *Storge* (STOR-gay) is familial love. It is what parents feel for a child, or what a family feels for grandparents and cousins. It is the affection born of the common bond of family. *Eros* (EE-rohs), of course, is erotic, romantic love. It is love rooted in attraction, desire, and—in marriage—the hope for sexual fulfillment. This love is God-given as both a gift to men and women and as one of the forces behind procreation and creating a legacy. Finally, there is *agape* (ah-GAH-peh). This is often described as the "God kind of love." The word refers to unconditional love. It is sacrificial love lavished upon someone by a decision rather than by any deserving behavior. It cannot be earned. It cannot be commanded. It is freely given and both undeserved and unconditional. It is the love Christ exercised when he died a gruesome death on a cross so that humanity might live.

While the first three help us understand the different ways we should respond to people in our relational spheres, the last creates the foundation that allows others to be whole and fulfilled. Unconditional love builds security in the object of its attention and, if everyone were to exercise it by giving it away, none would be without.

Agape makes both the giver and the recipient better. It sacrifices itself for the benefit of others. It rejoices in other's victories and laments over their loss. It does not rejoice when its enemy falls, but weeps for the pain and loss that did not have to be. *Agape* does not fail to accomplish what it set out to do and is not dependent on the object of its attention to judge its success. It requires nothing in return for its great sacrifices, and, when it receives, it creates pathways to unity and the common good. *Agape* is the force that makes reconciliation possible.

Drawing deeply from the *agape* stream by which it is planted, reconciliation allows the offended to care as much about the offender as he does himself, dissolving barriers to relationship, while building pathways of hope. It is *the* answer no one is looking for. It is also *the* answer for the racial crises and agonies of our time.

My young friends, this is what I want to hear. Seek *agape*. This is nearly the same thing as telling you to seek God. He is the source of this unconditional love that has the potential to change the world. Whatever your calling, whatever battles you have to fight for justice, live in agape. Strive for reconciliation. We must stop the unending tug-of-war that dominates our society now. Somebody has to step up. Somebody has to inject a new and cleansing force into our society. This force is *agape*, God is its source, and you are meant to be the conductors for our age. Hold this truth tightly and live it well. You are my generations' great hope.

Now, we must be clear-eyed about what is ahead for us. One would be hard-pressed to find a nation whose peoples have not struggled over power, influence, and resources. Invariably, greed motivates one ethnic group to diminish the value of another. Horrific acts are whitewashed so that innocence can be proclaimed, and ethnic division becomes a generational curse. Throughout time, antipathy grows to the point that both sides vilify the other for atrocities committed. There are usually two strategies employed at these moments: legislative pressure and sociological upheaval. Historically, both options have been effective at accomplishing their goals. Governments have been overthrown, and laws have been created that restrict people's misdeeds. Thus, if the goal is simply to restrain the lawless, or to shed more blood than our enemy does, then I think humanity can say, "mission accomplished!"

Here we sit, then, enjoying the temporary benefits won by the sword and the pen. Black and white Americans have lived through four hundred years of ethnic division. A civil war was fought. Laws have been created and constitutions have been amended, yet we are no further down the road to true healing, to true unity, to true reconciliation.

We are no closer to fixing our problems because we are using solutions that address the effects of our systemic issues, not the systemic issues themselves. Let me tell a story that might help us understand this better. If you were to walk with me from the family room in my home to our backyard, we would cross a deck leading to a set of twelve stairs. Not long ago, and after fifteen years of living in my home, I noticed that the first step on the staircase had begun to droop to one side. When we laid a level on the step, the bubble moved to the far end. I called a handyman to see what needed to be done. I suggested to him that we place a wooden support (a shim) underneath that sloping stair to lift it back to horizontal—an inexpensive fix. To my dismay, the handyman said, "You have a much bigger problem. The ground underneath the stairs has begun to sink, which is causing the footers to sink, and thus the entire staircase to sink. To repair the one angled stair, the foundation must be lifted by replacing the footers. Afterward, we can then address the years of damage done to each stair by the faulty foundation."

Ouch! I had to admit, he made sense. It all sounded right, but his solution was going to cost much more than a few shims. To fix the damage of years, I painfully paid the price for the repairs to be made.

It is the same with our country. Fearing the cost, America has chosen not to employ the one solution that will ensure justice, equality, and more. She has chosen not to build upon the mandate to love people as God loves us. Instead she opted to use lawmaking and sociological reform as substitutes for God's best. Yet all thinking people know that laws don't restrain the criminal, amendments don't transform a bigot, and civil conflict only embitters the loser. Legislation is vitally important, as is the responsibility to defend the oppressed. Corrupt rules must be amended. Bad legislation needs to be changed and misguided judicial precedent needs to be overturned. But it is more important that these initiatives be launched from a nation whose heart and people have been transformed by God's love; indeed, a people who have chosen reconciliation as the primary means by which they choose to chart a pathway to wholeness and peace.

Referring back to my home construction need, after years of trying to repair our national stairs with shims to get them even, it is time for us to approach the larger issue with the right solution. Loving people according to the gospel of Jesus Christ will cost more than any of us want to pay, but it is the best solution to address our unstable foundation.

Ethnic reconciliation fulfills the hope for which generations of abolitionists, enslaved Africans, civil rights activists, and good citizens strove. It will allow the ethnic differences which have historically divided us to instead unite us. It will help us value those different from us as a different kind of good, not a different kind of bad. It will help us forgive, and to offer meaningful apologies. It will heal us, not just bandage us.

Like Dr. King, I too have a dream. My dream is tailored to incorporate such a deep care for the black and white man that a twenty-second century, would-be American civil rights activist will have a hard time finding a job. There will be no need. The pain and the sting of injustice will have abated. The inequality will have been set right. True reconciliation will have long before come to reign in our land. And that divinely-granted *agape* love will permeate our institutions and our lives.

Now this can only happen if you, a young generation on the rise, are willing to stand on the shoulders of your ancestors and carry a new spirit into the tensions of where you are now. The old ways, I'm sorry to tell you, won't always work. The demands, the insistences, the ongoing tug-of-war—it hasn't produced what we've hoped for and it won't produce what we dream of in the future. We are going to have to ask God for an *agape* love that changes hearts, and then be willing to engage our adversaries in a new manner so as to win them as advocates in our cause.

I know that you are the generation of destiny who can bring this about. I know you are the ones who can light your torch from the life of Dr. King and Medgar Evers and Ralph Abernathy and Rosa Parks and John Lewis and a million other brave hearts who lived lives of wisdom, nonviolence, and love for all.

May our God fill you and guide you. May he give you courage and strength. May he make you mighty warriors against the spiritual forces that reinforce the natural forces of racism and hate. And may he give you a glorious day of victory that means freedom for generations yet unborn. My generation is with you. I am with you. Go, now, and change our world for God, for good, and forever.

CHAPTER 7

EPILOGUE

have been speaking in this book of forces—attitudes, beliefs, bitterness, and hatreds—that have perverted human souls and caused great suffering. These are products of natural experience. They are the imprint of history. Yet I want to end this book by describing a less natural force that can come upon a people. I think this may be happening in our time. In illustrating it and thus attempting to explain it, I want to use an episode that happened in our church while this book was being written.

I'm going to change the names in retelling this story. I will also blur some of the broader facts for the same reason. I do this only to protect the privacy of those involved. Yet you can trust me that the details are absolutely true. Everything happened just as described here.

It was a Saturday afternoon in the summer of 2020 when members of our staff were conducting a membership class we call "Life in the Spirit." It had been going on most of the day. The last moments had come and our leader for this seminar, we'll call him Jonathan, was just inviting the audience to a moment of prayer and ministry.

As this was going on, a young man who we'll call Jack entered the sanctuary where the seminar was being held. Jack had been involved in our church for several years though he had never become a member. When he entered the room, some of our staff and some of those attending the seminar noticed him. A few wondered why he was there. He had already completed this seminar some time before.

More than one person who saw him later said they knew there was something wrong. It was Jack, certainly, but he didn't look like himself. He was different in a dark and disturbing way. Beyond this, he had a pool cue in his hand. We would later learn that he also had a concealed knife.

He sat halfway down one of the main aisles in the 1500-seat sanctuary and positioned himself in an aisle seat. He listened for a moment while Jonathan began giving instructions to the seminar attendants. A time of prayer was next.

You should know that Jonathan is a fine African American man who leads both our ministry to men and many of our prayer ministries in the church. In fact, he is one of our foremost intercessory prayer warriors. There is no better way to say it than that he is a gift to our spiritual family.

As Jonathan was just beginning to pray, Jack rose from his seat. He began walking toward Jonathan. He also began yelling. It sounded like gibberish to most of those in the room. Though the details are a bit sketchy in the retelling—as often happens when traumatic events occur before a shocked crowd—it was then that Jack raised the pool cue, missing as he swung at Jonathan. Jonathon then grabbed Jack. In response, Jack raised his knife and stabbed our beloved leader in the chest.

Nearby, a husband and a wife, DeShawn and Donna, are sitting right where they've been sitting all day. When the horrific moment begins to unfold at the front of the room, the heroic Donna nudges her husband and tells him he should get up and go down there to help. He is already in motion as she finishes her sentence. DeShawn races to the front and jumps on Jack to restrain him. In the fight that follows, DeShawn is stabbed in the leg. The knife cuts into an artery. Blood begins spurting as from a hose.

Jonathan starts trying to defend DeShawn. He's been stabbed but fortunately the knife has skidded across his sternum and rib cage rather than piercing deeply. He knows, though, that DeShawn is in real danger. He can see the blood spurting and he knows he needs to help.

The whole scene is terrifying and threatening. As Jonathon attempts to move toward the foyer, Jack pursues him with knife in hand. In frustration, Jack throws the knife at Jonathon. He misses. Jonathon, seeing Jack without a weapon, musters the strength to tackle Jack. Pinning him down, he holds him until another attendee of the class relieved him, restraining the assailant. That attendee was the police chief of our county. He was in attendance that day putting the final touches on his membership with our church. Thank God he was there, because no one knew more about what should be done than him. Employing all his years of training, he engages Jack.

Now, Chief is in great shape and is quite strong. He reported later, though, that he was barely able to hold the much smaller Jack down. He remembers thinking that the kid had supernatural strength. He also remembers thinking, "I can't lose this fight. Other people will be in danger. I may have to kill this guy."

It was at that moment that the chief had an impression fill his mind. It was, "Do not kill this man." Heeding this impression, Chief started using non-life-threatening tactics to subdue Jack. Soon after, other police showed up. Jack was handcuffed and taken into custody.

Still, we had two wounded, and a police chief who was battered. The two stab victims were sped off to the hospital. DeShawn would undergo surgery and emerge just fine. Jonathan was checked, bandaged, and released the next day. That's when the problems began. To put days of agony into a few short sentences, an infection set in—probably from the shallow knife wounds—and Jonathan almost died. Thank God, the prayer of God's people and the skilled care of hospital staff returned him to us. He's a thriving member of our team to this day.

Now, I know this is a dramatic tale to tell, particularly at the end of a book rather than at the beginning. I understand if you need a moment to digest it all. Yet here is what I want you to remember if you forget every other detail of this episode in the years to come. We now know that as he was approaching Jonathan with the pool cue and the knife, Jack was accusing our pastor of having an affair with his wife. He was also insisting that Jonathan had abused his children. He kept making these accusations after he was in police custody. In fact, days later, Jack said he felt completely justified attacking Jonathan, given the affair and the abuse of his children.

Here's what you need to know. Jack doesn't have a wife. He doesn't have any children.

I have thought about this long and deeply. A white man attempted to kill a black man. That white man is divorced from reality. The police later reported that Jack was having a "psychotic episode." Yet this assailant alleges an affair with "his" woman, also alleges abuse of "his" children, and is filled with such unnatural strength that a seasoned police chief uses the word "supernatural" to describe it.

By conveying this insight, I am not attempting to contextualize this assault within the boundaries of a hate crime. I would not "cry wolf" if one wasn't present. Still, I should remind you of what allegations by a white man that a black man in some way lusted after or abused his woman have meant in American history. The mere suspicion of such a thing got Emmett Till hanged and beaten beyond recognition in 1955. The allegations later were proven to be lies. The same kind of suspicions, also unfounded, led to the entire Tulsa Race Massacre—one of the most ghastly and devastating episodes in American racial history—in 1921.

It seems to me that there was an outside strength and intelligence behind Jack on that spring Saturday afternoon. He had physical power beyond his own. He accused our pastor of just the kind of behavior that has incited race hate and violence for centuries. He did not back down in his charges even afterward, though nothing he believed could possibly have been true.

Perhaps you see where I am going with this. I'm a Christian. There is no evidence to suggest that Jack was a bigot, nor is there any reason to believe that he was intent on stopping the Gospel of Jesus Christ from being preached, but one does not have to be intentionally hateful, or a Gospel opponent to believe and act on a lie.

Being a pastor, I am mindful of spiritual powers, both the power of God and of the kingdom of darkness. There are those that are intent on stopping the progress of the Gospel and those whose have as their aim to bring increase division among ethnicities. I am of the opinion that both were at play on this tragic day.

I am not implying that Jack was somehow "demon possessed" when he launched his attack. That said, I do believe there were spiritual influences manipulating the timing of his act and the strength employed to accomplish it. The branding of his act has been legally defined as a psychotic event - and I completely understand why our police use such language- but allow me to add a different system of reference. Though my team and I will pray to see Jack restored, I have little doubt that multiple dark forces of evil were at work on that terrible day.

Here's where I want you to go with me. I believe dark forces are behind the sin of bigotry and racism. Those forces can move individuals and entire groups to hate, to racism and to violence and to lies? If true, then we have a two-tiered battle, a fight at two levels. We must contend with love and legislation the forces I've spent most of this book talking about—the bitterness, the race hate and the toxic cultures and the abuse. Yet I think we see in the story I've just told that that there is a spiritual battle we must also fight. We have to take a prayerful stand against those invisible but powerful battalions that work behind the scenes. They are there at a Klan rally. They were there when Emmett Till was hanged. They move skinheads to spew their hatred of blacks on America's streets. They may even feed the divisions among God's people.

I know this is a stretch for some of you who have stuck with me to this point. That's fine. Let the modern day labels of psychosis and shared delusional disorder scratch the itch that a natural cause demands. Yet understand that what I am describing is a force, whatever its name, that has pervaded our history. It is the mind-set behind the mind, the strategy behind the dark history. And those who are spiritually inclined must wisely, assertively, prayerfully and in the love of God approach it at every level in order to fashion that new day of justice, harmony, and full reconciliation.

Jonathan has recovered. DeShawn also. We are praying for Jack and will do what we can to help him with what he needs. I expect to see good things come from his life in time. Yet America is not well yet. It is not free of the lies or the bitterness or the violence or the hate. That day is coming. We are going to win that day together. We are going to change history by first changing the spiritual complexion of our lives and our times. May God grant it. May his will be done on earth as it is being done in heaven.

Walk in love. Kneel in humility. Serve with the strength God provides. Speak the truth with compassion. Care for your enemy and do not rejoice when he fails. Be the difference you are trying to create.

Let us set ourselves to the task.

BRETT FULLER

Pastor Brett Fuller is the Senior Pastor of Grace Covenant Church in Chantilly, Virginia, a suburb of Washington, DC. He currently serves as Chaplain of the Washington Football Team.

From 2005 to 2014, he served as Chaplain for the National Association of Basketball Coaches. In 2000, he inspired a bill in Congress to establish a memorial honoring the African American slaves who helped build America. Though the bill was never passed, he still seeks to complete this mission. In addition, from 2007 to 2009, he served on President George W. Bush's Advisory Board for Historically Black Colleges and Universities.

Pastor Brett has written two devotionals: *Live Well* and *Relate Well*. He and his lovely bride Cynthia were wed in December of 1986, and frequently conduct marriage and family seminars. Brett also coordinates relational and professional development seminars, helping leaders in every walk of life improve their craft. The Fullers reside in Chantilly,

Virginia, have parented seven children, and have been blessed with two wonderful daughters-in-law and one grandchild, Ava Lily.